Women's
Voices

Women's Voices

A DOCUMENTARY
HISTORY OF WOMEN
IN AMERICA

VOLUME 2:
Property
Equality
Reproduction

Edited by Lorie Jenkins McElroy

UXL®

AN IMPRINT OF GALE

DETROIT · NEW YORK · TORONTO · LONDON

Women's Voices:
A Documentary History of Women in America

Lorie Jenkins McElroy, Editor

Staff

Elizabeth Des Chenes, *U·X·L Developmental Editor*
Carol DeKane Nagel, *U·X·L Managing Editor*
Thomas L. Romig, *U·X·L Publisher*

Kim Smilay, *Permissions Specialist*

Shanna P. Heilveil, *Production Assistant*
Evi Seoud, *Assistant Production Manager*
Mary Beth Trimper, *Production Director*

Pamela A. E. Galbreath, *Art Director*
Cynthia Baldwin, *Product Design Manager*

Linda Mahoney, *Typesetting*

Library of Congress Cataloging-in-Publication Data

Women's Voices : a documentary history of women in America
/ edited by Lorie Jenkins McElroy
    p. cm.
    Includes bibliographical references and index.

    Contents: v. 1. Education, abolition, suffrage – v. 2. Equality, property,
reproduction

    ISBN 0-7876-0663-4 (set: acid-free paper). – ISBN 0-7876-0664-2
(v. 1: acid-free paper). – ISBN 0-7876-0665-0 (v. 2: acid-free paper)

    1. Women–United States–History–Sources. 2. Women's Rights–
United States–History–Sources. I. McElroy, Lorie Jenkins.

    HQ1410.W688   1996
    305.4'0973–dc20

                                                                    96-25579
                                                                    CIP

Printed in the United States of America

10 9 8 7 6 5 4 3 2 1

Contents

Bold type indicates volume number
Regular type indicates page number

Lucretia Mott

v

Abolition

Property and Labor

Civic and Social Equality

Reader's Guide

Women's Voices: A Documentary History of Women in America presents 32 original documents that trace the development of women's rights in America from the Revolutionary War to the present. The speeches, diary entries, newspaper articles, poems, and reminiscences featured in these two volumes explore a number of movements that influenced the crusade for equal rights, including education and labor reform, social equality, and women's suffrage. Activists such as Susan B. Anthony and Sojourner Truth and their works may be recognizable to readers; perhaps less familiar are figures such as Sarah Bagley, who wrote about female workers during the early days of the Industrial Revolution, and Alice Paul, who proposed the first Equal Rights Amendment in 1923. While the majority of entries reflect a feminine perspective, prominent male supporters of women's rights—such as Frederick Douglass—are also represented. In studying the original documents presented in *Women's Voices,* users can gain a unique perspective of how individuals—many of whom risked a great deal to present their views—helped shape the past and influence the present.

Frances E. Willard

Format

Both *Women's Voices* volumes are divided into three chapters. Each of the six chapters focus on a specific theme: Education, Abolition, Suffrage, Labor, Social Equality, and Reproductive Rights. Every chapter opens with an historical overview, followed by four to seven document excerpts.

Each excerpt is divided into six sections:

- **Introductory material** places the document and its author in an historical context

- **Things to Remember** offers readers important background information about the featured text

- **Excerpt** presents the document in its original language and format

- **What happened next** discusses the impact of the document on both the speaker and his or her audience

- **Did you know** provides interesting facts about each document and its author

- **For Further Reading** presents sources for more information on documents and speakers

Additional Features

Every *Women's Voices* entry contains a speaker's biographical box, call-out boxes examining related events and issues, and black-and-white illustrations. Each excerpt is accompanied by a glossary running alongside the primary document that defines terms and ideas. Both volumes contain a timeline of important events and cumulative index.

Acknowledgments

Special thanks are due for the invaluable comments and suggestions provided by U·X·L's women's books advisors:

Annette Haley, High School Librarian/Media Specialist at Grosse Ile High School in Grosse Ile, Michigan; Mary Ruthsdotter, Projects Director of the National Women's History Project; Francine Stampnitzky, Children's/Young Adult Librarian at the Elmont Public Library in Elmont, New York; and Ruth Ann

Karlin Yeske, Librarian at North Middle School in Rapid City, South Dakota.

Thanks also go to the Butler Library at Columbia University, the collections staff at Barnard College and Rutgers University, the reference librarians in Union, New Jersey, and researcher Donald Sauvigne. Added acknowledgment goes to Mary Bell, Robert Frauenhoff, and Lynn Mandon at Wayne Hills High School in Wayne, New Jersey.

Comments and Suggestions

We welcome your comments and suggestions for documents to feature in future editions of *Women's Voices*. Please write: Editor, *Women's Voices,* U·X·L, 835 Penobscot Bldg., Detroit, Michigan, 48226-4094; call toll free: 1-800-347-4253; or fax: 313-961-6348.

Preface

When we learn about history from a biography or textbook, our understanding of events and people is colored by an historian's interpretation of the past. When we read primary source documents such as the 32 pieces found in *Women's Voices,* however, we can interpret history for ourselves. The accounts and perspectives in these speeches, diaries, essays, and letters open a unique and very personal window on the past, reminding us that we all make history a little bit every day.

The entries in *Women's Voices* show that women have long shaped historical events (even when their personal stories were written in invisible ink). Through reviewing these primary sources in their historical context, readers discover the vital role American women played in the ongoing fight for equal rights, a fight that often took heavy personal tolls. Readers will learn about the hopes and dreams women held for their families, communities, and country and how these dreams helped shape current social and political trends. The women featured in *Voices* come from differing time periods, backgrounds, and social

Charlotte Perkins Gilman

spheres, yet they are joined by a common bond: the desire to improve the status of *all* women through a variety of means, including education, political activism, and legal reform.

The *Voices* documents—presented whenever possible in their original format—reveal that there was often disagreement about how change should (and would) come about. In some cases, major philosophical differences turned woman against woman; in other instances, unexpected alliances were formed, some of which included men. Many of the women featured in *Voices* saw frustratingly little progress towards equality during their lifetimes—most, in fact, were widely criticized for speaking their minds. While change was slow, progress was eventually made—especially with regard to women's suffrage. Women in today's America have a greater voice than in any period of the country's history. For this, they can thank their predecessors who, through the strength of their own words and beliefs, created a climate where change could be realized.

Mary Ruthsdotter, Projects Coordinator
National Women's History Project
May, 1996

Property and Labor

Jane Addams

Since colonial times American women have contributed to the well-being of their families on the domestic front. But as the impact of the Industrial Revolution (a time of massive mechanical innovation and economic change) swept across the country early in the nineteenth century, women began to work outside of the home. Technological advances—especially in the harnessing of water and steam power—created entirely new industries that needed many new workers. More and more factories began to dot the landscape and attract thousands of workers from rural areas.

In 1822 an enterprising group of businessmen started an industrial community in Lowell, Massachusetts, specializing in textile manufacturing. The entrepreneurs decided to staff the mills with young single women and pay them up to $3.00 per week, which was one-half the rate for skilled male workers at the time. Thousands of women, including **Sarah G. Bagley**, left their farm homes to work in the Lowell mills. Bagley and other young women wrote about their experiences in the *Lowell Offer-*

ing, the only magazine operated entirely by mill workers. In 1845 she and other "mill girls" formed the Lowell Female Labor Reform Association to protest poor working conditions and to lobby for a ten-hour workday.

While single women in Lowell struggled to improve their working conditions, married women also faced considerable challenges. Due to the influence of English common law, which settlers brought with them to the American colonies, women lost their legal rights when they married. A married woman gave up control of her own property and wages and could not even represent herself in legal matters. During the 1840s **Ernestine L. Rose** traveled throughout New York State in support of a bill that would protect the rights and property of married women. A powerful and persuasive speaker, she influenced many listeners and helped win passage of the first married women's property act in 1848.

Following the American Civil War, the Industrial Revolution gained momentum, creating enormously powerful and wealthy industries in transportation, banking, steel, and oil. At the height of this era, **Charlotte Perkins Gilman** suggested in her famous book, *Women and Economics*, that women would not be able to achieve equality in industrial society while they remained economically dependent on men. Gilman encouraged women to shed the chains of domestic life and become paid professionals and skilled laborers. She also suggested revolutionary concepts, including day care for children and "kitchen-less homes," so women could venture outside of the home and share equally in the advantages of the industrial age.

A few years later **Jane Addams** began voicing her concern with the plight of poor immigrants. Addams promoted the idea of education and assistance for struggling immigrant families to help them assimilate into American society. In the poor slums of Chicago, she established Hull House, a place where immigrants could learn English, practice their faith, and find decent living accommodations safe from greedy landlords and crime. In her book *Twenty Years at Hull House*, Addams discusses the benefits of a comprehensive learning environment to help all those in need, including young children and the elderly. The "settlement house" movement soon spread across the country and grew to include over four hundred centers that provided education, civic improvement, and community support for the urban poor.

During the early twentieth century factory owners were notorious for exploiting their employees. Laborers were forced to put up with unsafe working environments, unreasonable rules and regulations, long hours, and poor wages. Because of these horrible working conditions, some factories came to be called "sweatshops."

In 1911 the **Triangle Shirtwaist Factory Fire** in New York City profoundly influenced the labor movement's effort to improve the lives of the working class. After having fought off the employees' attempt to unionize, the owners of Triangle Shirtwaist locked the doors of their high-rise factory in order to keep out labor organizers. When a fire broke out on the eighth floor one Saturday afternoon, many workers jumped from windows to their deaths because they could not escape through the locked doors. This tragedy prompted the development of building and fire codes that continue to protect workers today.

During World War II American industrial output became highly dependent on women who built airplanes and ammunition and worked in the armed services to support the Allied war effort. Women's contributions helped influence the outcome of the war and forever opened the doors of opportunity to many types of employment. One of the most prominent women of the post-depression and World War II era was First Lady **Eleanor Roosevelt**, the wife of President Franklin Delano Roosevelt. She helped ensure that New Deal work programs provided economic opportunity for blacks as well as women as the nation recovered from the Great Depression. In recognition of her leadership abilities, President John F. Kennedy appointed her to head the Commission on the Status of Women in 1961. The commission's report, *American Women*, was published after her death in 1963, but its findings became part of the most sweeping civil rights legislation in American history. The resultant Equal Pay Act of 1963 mandated the idea of "equal pay for equal work" and became the first federal legislation of any kind to specifically prohibit discrimination on the basis of gender.

The following year Congress enacted the Civil Rights Act of 1964, which guaranteed equal opportunity in hiring practices and prohibited all forms of discrimination. The federal government set up the Equal Employment Opportunity Commission to assure that businesses and industry would comply with the law. Shortly thereafter President Lyndon Baines Johnson ordered that businesses actively seek out minorities and women in their recruiting and hiring practices, a concept called "affirmative action."

More recently, women workers won protection from sexual harassment under the provisions of the Civil Rights Act of 1991. In addition, the Family and Medical Leave Act of 1993 assures that all workers, both women and men, can attend to family emergencies without fear of losing their jobs.

Tales of Factory Life, No. 2: The Orphan Sisters

A selection from The Lowell Offering
Written by Sarah G. Bagley
Originally published in 1841

In 1822 a group of businessmen launched an ambitious and unusual plan to build an entire community centered around the milling (manufacturing) industry. They chose a site near the Merrimack and Concord rivers in Massachusetts and established the Merrimack Manufacturing Corporation as the first of 19 mills. The investors named the new community "Lowell" after their recently deccased business partner Francis Cabot Lowell, who had introduced the English power loom to America in 1817. The enterprise would become famous as the nation's first planned industrial community and as one of the early sites of the female labor movement in America.

The Lowell factory owners decided to staff their mills with female employees and offered salaries between $1.85 and $3.00 per week, the highest wages ever available to women workers. These salaries allowed the owners considerable savings since male mill workers typically received wages twice as high. The owners needed to ensure the overall well-being of their female

employees in order to persuade New England farmers to allow their daughters to move to Lowell and work at the factories. "Mill girls" were required to live in company-owned boarding-houses and obey strict rules such as nightly curfews and attendance at church on Sundays.

In 1836 a woman named Sarah G. Bagley left her home in New Hampshire and went to work for the Hamilton Company, one of the mills in Lowell. Bagley, like many other mill girls, studied at night and attended lectures on the weekends to better her education. She also became a regular contributor to the magazine *Lowell Offering,* edited by two former mill workers, Harriet F. Farley and Harriot Curtis. Unlike other magazines of its type, the *Lowell Offering* did not accept stories written by male factory owners. In fact, the publication's banner described it as "A Repository of Original Articles, Written Exclusively by Females Actively Employed in the Mills." Much to the delight of the mill owners the magazine won praise from both Americans and Europeans. It represented the best possible result of industrial enterprise—young women earning decent wages and "improving" themselves.

Shortly after Bagley wrote "The Orphan Sisters," she and other mill workers started the Lowell Female Labor Reform Association in 1845. Frustrated by the poor working conditions, extended work hours, and threats of reduced pay, the women dedicated their efforts to secure a ten-hour workday. The association grew rapidly under the leadership of Bagley, who traveled to nearby towns to lecture and establish similar groups of female workers.

Things to Remember While Reading "The Orphan Sisters":

- The mill factories of Lowell offered many New England farm girls the first real chance to work for regular wages. The characters in Bagley's story do not have any other options for working to support themselves and their family.

- Like the character Catherine B., most mill girls worked for an average of four years before returning to their families, getting married, or changing careers.

- Many girls were overwhelmed at first by the bustling factory town of Lowell, which was very different from the rural areas they left. Boardinghouses gave the girls a secure and stable home while they learned the ways of working and living in Lowell.

The Triangle Shirtwaist Factory Fire

New York City, 1911

New York City's Triangle Shirtwaist Factory once employed nearly one thousand female garment workers and was located in the Asch Building in the busy neighborhood of Washington Square Park. In 1910 the company endured a long strike and successfully thwarted the workers' attempt to unionize. Once the strike ended and the women returned to work, the owners began locking the factory doors to prevent union organizers from entering and mingling with workers. The owners also locked certain areas to prevent workers from stealing from the inventory of valuable lace and linen fabric.

In February 1911 a U.S. Labor Department inspection found many unsafe conditions at Triangle's Asch Building factory. The inspector noticed the locked exits and a stairway to the street that was only 18 inches wide; he also noted that the exit doorways swung inward, making them difficult to open in a crowded situation. Oily rags and piles of flammable fabric lay strewn upon the floor, and cigarette stains marked the surfaces of cutting tables. While the inspector reported these observations, including the evidence of cigarette smoking, the Labor Department took no action.

March 25, 1911, was a Saturday, but at Triangle it was also payday. Instead of the normal workforce of nine hundred, only five hundred workers showed up for work. At 4:45 P.M., shortly after the managers distributed the payroll, a fire broke out on the eighth floor. When workers there could not contain the flames, they rang an alarm bell and then evacuated the building. However, the doors on the ninth floor were locked, which prevented the workers on that floor from escaping. The fire spread and eventually claimed the lives of 146 workers, some as young as 14 years old. Many women died when the flames forced them to jump from windows on the ninth floor to the sidewalk below. When the fire department arrived, it had no ladders to reach beyond the sixth floor; nets failed to catch the falling victims.

A committee, which was formed to investigate the cause of the tragedy, helped establish many new laws. Modern building and fire codes include strict specifications regarding water sprinklers and the design of doorways and stairs. The Triangle factory fire also propelled union activism in the United States—and especially in New York. The ILGWU (International Ladies Garment Workers Union), formed in 1910, grew to one of the most powerful forces in organized labor. Following the tragedy, Francis Perkins, a member of the investigating committee who later became President Franklin D. Roosevelt's labor secretary, proclaimed: "These workers did not die in vain and we will never forget them."

Tales of Factory Life, No. 2: The Orphan Sisters

Catherine B. was the eldest of three sisters. Actual misfortune placed her parents in such an embarrassed state of affairs, as to make it necessary for Catherine and a younger sister to support themselves at an early age. They had learned the **pecuniary** advantages of factory life, from some of their young friends who had returned from a neighboring village, where they had been employed in a cotton mill. They earnestly requested the leave of their parents to go to Lowell to seek their fortune, as they termed such an adventure. After some deliberation, they gave their consent, but not without much **solicitude** for their safety.

The evening previously to their departure, the family met around the altar of devotion, where, with the faltering voice of emotion, the **benediction** of Heaven was invoked in behalf of the sisters, who were about to leave the **paternal** home for a residence among strangers.

The next morning, the sisters left their much-loved home, to obtain a livelihood—and as they cast a wishful eye upon the friends they had left, a sadness stole unconsciously over their **buoyant** spirits, unknown to them before.

They arrived at their place of destination, and were successful in finding employment. But what a great contrast from the quiet country-home in the neighborhood of the White Mountains, was the City of Spindles, to the sisters! They had been accustomed to listen only to

> Nature's wild, unconscious song,
> O'er thousand hills that floats along."—

But here was confusion in all its forms; and truly, said Catherine, "I should like to find myself alone for a brief

Pecuniary: *About money.*
Solicitude: *Concern.*
Benediction: *Blessing.*
Paternal: *Their father's.*
Buoyant: *Cheerful.*

A woman weaves cloth at a power loom.

space, that I might hold **communion** with my own heart undisturbed."

Time soon rendered these scenes less annoying; and soon were our young friends able to fix their attention upon any subject within their range of thought, with the **multitude** around them.

Nothing of much importance occurred during their first year's stay in Lowell; only they wrote often to their friends, and received letters from them often in return, **abounding** in such advice as their friends thought might be useful to them, under the circumstances in which they were placed. They were requested to return in one year from the time they left, and visit their friends, and had made their arrangements to be absent a few weeks, when a message was received from their mother for them to return as soon as possible, as their father was dangerously ill.

Communion: *Sharing thoughts or feelings.*
Multitude: *Masses of people.*
Abounding: *Filled.*

Bagley

Next morning they started, and arrived the day following. Their mother met them at the door, with the sad **intelligence** that their father could survive but a few hours at most. He was very weak, and could only give them a few words of advice; and then bade them a long farewell.

Their mother was nearly exhausted with fatigue; and constant watching had rendered her health very low. She was attacked by a like disease, and survived their father but a few weeks. The same grave opened to receive her, that had been prepared for their father, and these sisters were truly orphans.

Could this sad tale of suffering end here, the deep feelings of sympathy might be spared the reader, in a good measure; but there are other scenes too interesting to leave without notice.—A little brother and sister are here, and what shall be done with them? Catherine was to take charge of them, by special request from her mother, in her last moments. But how to provide for them a home, was what most troubled her. The advice of friends was cheap: every one would **bestow** it **gratuitously**—and there were as many opinions as persons. Some gave it as their opinion, that it might be proper to throw them on the public charity; but to this, Catherine replied, with her usual decision—"Give them into the care of strangers! No. I will work till I die, before I will consent to such a course. If any one must suffer **privation**, let it fall on me, and not on these children, who have not yet learned that the cup of human existence is mixed with bitterness and sorrow."

After having heard various opinions, they thought proper to ask advice of one who had **manifested** much kindness in their time of trouble—and he gave it as his opinion, that it would be well to **board** their little brother in a good family in the neighborhood, and take their sister with them to Lowell—to which they consented. The little furniture, and what else that remained, was disposed of, to settle some trifling debts that would unavoidably be contracted under the circumstances in which they were placed; and only a few things were reserved

Intelligence: *News.*

Bestow: *To present as a gift or honor.*

Gratuitously: *Freely.*

Privation: *Lack of basic comforts of life.*

Manifested: *Demonstrated.*

Board: *To reside in a home or place where meals are provided for a fee.*

by them as a memorial of the past. And as they gave the last fond farewell to the home of their earliest years, how sad and dejected were the once buoyant spirits of the sisters!

*A kind neighbor bade them welcome to his house as their home during their short stay, and assisted them in arranging their affairs, by **procuring** a boarding-place for their brother, and rendering them such other assistance as they needed. The evening previously to their departure, Catherine went to the place sacred to memory, where lay the slumbering dust of all that we claim as friends, under all circumstances. It was a lone, dreary spot. **Nought** but the **plaintive** notes of the **whippoorwill**, and the waving branches of the willow, were heard to break the silence of evening. She sat down upon a stone, near the quiet resting place of those loved friends, and gave full vent to the sorrowful emotions of her heart. She felt that there is a power to soothe in holding communion with the dead; and most fervently did she pray, that she might be strengthened to fulfil the duties of a mother to those little ones, who had been left in her care by the death of her parents.*

Next day, the sisters started again for Lowell; but not with the same thoughts and feelings as when they left before. They left now with the gloomy reflection that they had no home—no friends on whom they could rely, if sick or unfortunate; and in their care was a little sister; and a brother still younger, whose board they were under obligation to pay, they had left behind.

They arrived safely in Lowell, and with heavy hearts; for they thought it would be difficult for them to procure board for a child so young. They consulted a lady of their acquaintance, who very kindly offered to board her; and look after her, during their absence in the mill.... How abundant is the satisfaction of that kind-hearted woman, in having contributed so much to relieve the heavy burdens of those orphan sisters!

Heaven smiled upon their efforts, and good health and prosperity have attended them; but no one can suppose, for a moment, that they have not possessed a self-sacrificing spirit.

Procuring: Acquiring.
Nought: Nothing.
Plaintive: Sorrowful; mournful.
Whippoorwill: Brownish North American bird that is active at night.

Sarah G. Bagley

While not many details are known about Sarah G. Bagley's life before and after her involvement with labor activities in Lowell, historians believe she was born in Meredith, New Hampshire. In 1845 Bagley co-organized the Lowell Female Labor Reform Association, which petitioned the Massachusetts State Legislature to enact a ten-hour workday. Around the same time she served as corresponding secretary of the New England Workingmen's Association and frequently wrote articles for the group's magazine, *Voice of Industry*. Bagley also started the Industrial Reform Lyceum, a speakers' program that brought labor activists to Lowell. In 1846 she served as a delegate to the National Industrial Congress, an early national labor organization, and helped lead a second unsuccessful movement for a ten-hour workday.

The little sister was kept at school, until she was old enough to earn her living, with a little assistance; and then she was sent into the country, to reside with a friend, and go to school a part of the time. The little brother is able to earn his living six months in the year, and the sisters furnish means to keep him at school the remainder.

*But let no one suppose that the care of these children has diminished the real happiness of the sisters—for they assured me it was a rich source of pleasure to review the past, and call to mind the many times when they were obliged to spend all but a few shillings, in providing for those little ones. "And," said Catherine, "it has taught me lessons of practical **benevolence**; for I have seen the time when it would cost an effort to give half a dollar, be its object ever so praiseworthy."*

The sisters have of late been able to lay by a small sum for themselves—thereby evincing the utility of perseverance in well-doing; and though it may seem to many that their lot has been a hard one, still they are blest with sunshine and flowers;

Benevolence: Acting kindly.

and when next you see Catherine's name, it shall be in the list of marriages. S. G. B. (Bagley in Eisler, pp. 70-73)

What happened next...

The Lowell Female Labor Reform Association organized a petition drive requesting the Massachusetts Legislature to enact a ten-hour workday law. As a result, the Massachusetts lawmakers conducted the first ever government investigation into labor conditions; still, they declined to recommend a ten-hour workday in their final report.

Bagley successfully showed the potential of women as a collective bargaining force in labor. Shortly after 1845 factory owners began boarding new female workers individually instead of in group homes to prevent networking. The arrival of Irish immigrants to the United States in the 1840s provided a new source of cheap labor for the mill owners and marked the end of the Lowell chapter in America's history of organized female labor.

Did you know...

- The social and industrial community experiment in Lowell attracted worldwide attention. Many famous people, including British authors Charles Dickens and Anthony Trollope, traveled to Massachusetts to observe firsthand the lives of the female factory mill workers.

- The magazine *Lowell Offering* enjoyed immense popularity even beyond America. Harriet Martineau, a leading British historian, helped publish an anthology of *Offering* writings called *Mind Among the Spindles* in 1844.

- Despite her poor health from working in the mills for nine years, Bagley began a new career for herself in 1846 as the first female telegraph operator in America.

For Further Reading

Eisler, Benita, ed. *The Lowell Offering: Writings by New England Mill Women (1840-1845)*. Philadelphia: J. B. Lippincott, 1977.

Josephson, Hannah. *The Golden Threads: New England's Mill Girls and Magnates*. New York: Duell, Sloan & Pierce, 1949.

Stern, Madeleine B. *We, the Women: Career Firsts of Nineteenth Century America*. New York: Schulte Publishing Company, 1963.

The Broadway Tabernacle speech

September 7, 1853

A letter to Susan B. Anthony

January 9, 1877

Selections from writings by Ernestine L. Rose

English settlers brought many customs with them to the American colonies, including their legal traditions. Under the system of English "common law," women lost their legal rights when they married. The famous British law authority Sir William Blackstone explained the legality of marriage known as *coverture:* "By marriage, the husband and wife are one person in law: that is, the very being or legal existence of the woman is suspended during the marriage, or at the very least is incorporated and consolidated into that of the husband; under whose wing, protection, and *cover,* she performs everything." Blackstone's 1765 book *Commentaries on the Laws of England* served as the primary source of legal guidance even after the American Revolution. As individual states created their own property and inheritance laws, they continued to limit the rights of married women based on this tradition of English common law.

In 1836 Judge Thomas Herttell, a member of the New York State Legislature, introduced a bill to protect the rights and property of married women. His proposed bill attempted to correct the existing statutes in New York State that severely denied married women legal rights. According to those laws, a married woman lost control of her own property and wages and could not represent herself in legal matters. Also, if her husband died without a will, she was not entitled to all of their possessions. Herttell's proposed bill, which sought to change these rules, caught the attention of Ernestine L. Rose, a woman who would lead the fight for its passage over the next 12 years.

Ernestine and her husband, William E. Rose, arrived in America from England in 1836, the same year Judge Herttell first proposed his bill. In spite of her accent, the Polish-born Rose was a powerful speaker who had begun her lecturing career during the British labor movement earlier in the 1830s. Outraged by the substandard legal status granted to married women in the States, Rose traveled extensively throughout New York to win support for Herttell's bill. She drafted a petition urging the legislature to pass the bill and went door to door seeking signatures. The first year of hard work produced a meager handful of signatures. Undaunted, she continued year after year organizing petition drives and speaking before the State Assembly.

Finally, in 1848 "An Act for the More Effectual Protection of the Property of Married Women" became law in New York. While the passage of this bill represented a significant victory for women's rights, it did not fully secure the legal rights of married women. During the 1850s Rose continued trying to win comprehensive property rights for married women, such as the right to enter business contracts and to have equal custody of children in divorce cases.

Things to Remember While Reading Selections from Rose's Speech and Letter:

- Existing New York law specified exactly which household items widows were allowed to keep. By listing the actual points of the law, Rose shows its shortcomings and absurdities. Notice the audience laughs and hisses at various times during her speech.

- Rose argues that as laws become outdated they should be changed to reflect current circumstances. While the law in her time allowed women to keep their spinning wheels and weaving looms, the invention of steam-powered mills had made these items obsolete.

- In her letter to women's rights leader Susan B. Anthony, Rose mentions her countless trips across the country to deliver lectures. She wonders if she damaged her health by traveling so much and under such difficult conditions.

Speech Given at the Broadway Tabernacle, September 7, 1853

*Mrs. ROSE said: As to the personal property, after all debts and **liabilities** are discharged, the widow receives one-half of it; and, in addition, the law kindly allows her own wearing apparel, her own **ornaments**, proper to her station, one bed, with **appurtenances** for the same; a stove, the Bible, family pictures, and all the school-books; also, all spinning-wheels and weaving-looms, one table, six chairs, tea cups and saucers, one tea-pot, one sugar dish, and six spoons. (Much laughter). But the law does not inform us whether they are to be tea or table spoons; nor does the law make any provision for kettles, sauce-pans, and all such necessary things. But the **presumption** seems to be that the spoons meant are tea-spoons; for, as ladies are generally considered very delicate, the law presumed that a widow might live on tea only; but spinning-wheels and weaving-looms are very necessary articles for ladies nowadays. (Hissing and great confusion). Why, you need not hiss, for I am **expounding** the law. These wise law-makers, who seem to have lived somewhere about the **time of the flood**, did not dream of spinning and weaving by steam-power. When our great-great-grandmothers had to weave every article of apparel worn by the family, it was, no doubt, considered a very good law to allow the widow the*

Liabilities: Financial debts.

Ornaments: Accessories.

Appurtenances: Related accessories; in this case, things such as blankets and pillows.

Presumption: Assumption.

Expounding: Stating the facts.

Time of the flood: An expression meaning a long time ago; refers to the Old Testament biblical account of Noah, who at God's command built an ark that saved him, his family, and a pair of each animal from the great flood that covered the earth.

Protecting the Rights of Working Families

The dual demands of family and job place an enormous burden on working women and men. By the last quarter of the twentieth century many American families consisted of two wage earners, abandoning the stereotype of the "homemaker" mother and the working father. In addition, the traditional definition of "family" has changed dramatically over the years. Adult wage earners are often struggling to provide not only child care but care for their own aging parents as well. And single parent families, frequently headed by women, are especially concerned about job security and maintaining a stable income.

The Family and Medical Leave Act of 1993 is legislation designed to help working women and men address pressing personal needs without jeopardizing their jobs and income. The act requires employers with more than 50 employees to grant up to 12 weeks unpaid leave for workers to take care of pressing personal situations, such as adjusting to the birth or adoption of a child, the care of a family member with a serious medical condition, or an illness that prevents the employee from working. Under the terms of the Family and Medical Leave Act, an employer is required to restore the employee to his or her former position or to an equivalent position with equivalent pay and benefits. Furthermore the leave will not result in the loss of any employment benefits. The act also prevents employers from using an unfortunate or unplanned personal occurrence to their financial advantage—by, for instance, reducing or denying health benefits to an employee on leave.

possession of the spinning-wheels and the weaving-looms. But, unfortunately for some laws, man is a progressive being; his belief, opinions, habits, manners, and customs change, and so do spinning-wheels and weaving-looms; and, with men and things, law must change too, for what is the value of a law when man has outgrown it? As well might you bring him to the use of his baby clothes, because they once fitted him, as to keep him to such a law. No. Laws, when man has outgrown them, are fit only to be cast aside among the things that were.

But I must not forget, the law allows the widow something more. She is allowed one cow, all sheep to the number of ten, with the fleeces and the cloth from the same, two swine, and the pork therefrom. (Great laughter). My friends, do not say that I stand here to make these laws ridiculous. No; if you laugh, it is at their own **inherent ludicrousness**; for I state them simply and truly as they are; for they are so ridiculous in themselves, that it is impossible to make them more so. (Stanton et al., pp. 561-62)

Letter to Susan B. Anthony written from London, January 9, 1877

MY DEAR MISS ANTHONY:—Sincerely do I thank you for your kind letter. Believe me it would give me great pleasure to comply with your request, to tell you all about myself and my past labors; but I suffer so much from **neuralgia** in my head and general **debility**, that I could not undertake the task, especially as I have nothing to refer to. I have never spoken from notes; and as I did not intend to publish anything about myself, for I had no other ambition except to work for the cause of humanity, irrespective of sex, sect, country, or color, and did not expect that a Susan B. Anthony would wish to do it for me, I made no **memorandum** of places, dates, or names; and thirty or forty years ago the press was not sufficiently educated in the rights of woman, even to notice, much less to report speeches as it does now; and therefore I have not anything to assist me or you.

All that I can tell you is, that I used my humble powers to the uttermost, and raised my voice in behalf of Human Rights in general, and the elevation and Rights of Woman in particular, nearly all my life. And so little have I spared myself, or studied my comfort in summer or winter, rain or shine, day or night, when I had an opportunity to work for the cause to which I had devoted myself, that I can hardly wonder at my present state of health.

Inherent ludicrousness:
Essentially laughable or absurd in nature.

Neuralgia: A painful condition involving the nervous system.

Debility: Weakness.

Memorandum: A written reminder.

Ernestine L. Rose

Ernestine Louise Sismondi Potowski Rose (1810-1892), the only child of Rabbi Potowski and his wife, was born in the Jewish ghetto of Piotrkow in Poland. At 17 she left her native country and traveled on her own to Germany. After living in Germany, Holland, and France, Rose arrived in England in 1830 when she was 20 years old. She became active in the reform movement led by social philosopher Robert Owen, who was famous for improving working conditions for mill workers and their children. In 1836 she married William E. Rose, who was also a disciple of Owen. In America her eloquence as a public speaker won her the nickname "Queen of the Platform." She traveled extensively throughout the country speaking for women's rights, temperance (outlawing liquor production, sale, and consumption), and abolition (an end to slavery).

Yet in spite of hardships, for it was not as easy to travel at that time as now, and the expense, as I never made a charge or took up a collection, I look back to that time, when a stranger and alone, I went from place to place, in high-ways and by-ways, did the work and paid my bills with great pleasure and satisfaction; for the cause gained ground, and in spite of my **heresies** *I had always good audiences, attentive listeners, and was well received wherever I went.*

Heresies: Opinions that go against generally accepted beliefs.

But I can mention from memory the principal places where I have spoken. In the winter of 1836 and '37, I spoke in New York, and for some years after I lectured in almost every city in the State; Hudson, Poughkeepsie, Albany, Schenectady, Saratoga, Utica, Syracuse, Rochester, Buffalo, Elmira, and other places; in New Jersey, in Newark and Burlington; in 1837, in Philadelphia, Bristol, Chester, Pittsburg, and other places in Pennsylvania, and at Wilmington in Delaware; in 1842, in Boston, Charlestown, Beverly, Florence, Springfield, and other points in Massachusetts, and in Hartford, Connecticut; in 1844, in Cincinnati, Dayton, Zanesville, Springfield, Cleveland, Toledo, and several settlements in the backwoods of Ohio, and also in Richmond, Indiana; in 1845 and '46, I lectured three times in the Legislative Hall in Detroit, and at Ann Arbor and other places in Michigan; and in 1847 and '48, I spoke in Charleston and Columbia, in South Carolina.

In 1850, I attended the first National Woman's Rights Convention in Worcester [Massachusetts], and nearly all the National and State Conventions since, until I went to Europe in 1869. Returning to New York in 1874, I was present at the Convention in Irving Hall, the only one held during my visit to America.

I sent the first petition to the New York Legislature to give a married woman the right to hold real estate in her own name, in the winter of 1836 and '37, to which after a good deal of trouble I obtained five signatures. Some of the ladies said the gentlemen would laugh at them; others, that they had rights enough; and the men said the women had too many rights already. Woman at that time had not learned to know that she had any rights except those that man in his generosity allowed her; both have learned something since that time which they will never forget. I continued sending petitions with increased numbers of signatures until 1848 and '49, when the Legislature enacted the law which granted to woman the right to keep what was her own. But no sooner did *it become legal than all the women said, "Oh! that is right! We ought always to have had that."*

During the eleven years from 1837 to 1848, I addressed the New York Legislature five times, and since 1848 I can not say positively, but a good many times; you know all that better than any one else.

Your affectionate friend,
ERNESTINE L. ROSE
(Stanton et al., pp. 98-100)

What happened next...

In 1854 the women of New York held their annual state convention in Albany, the state capital. The convention lasted two weeks due to its surprising popularity with the public. Rose and other women leaders presented their arguments to the State Assembly for various legal reforms, including an extension of married women's rights. Even when the legislature denied their petitions, the women continued to hold their annual meetings in Albany. Finally in 1860 the New York State Legislature passed an "Act Concerning the Rights and Liabilities of Husband and Wife," which granted comprehensive rights to married women. The married women property acts passed in New York became the model for other states, with 29 states passing similar acts by the end of the Civil War.

Did you know...

- At age 16 Rose took her father to court when he arranged her marriage to an older man and offered the inheritance she had received from her mother as a dowry. She won back her inheritance but gave it to her father as a gift before leaving Poland in 1827.

- To support herself while living in Berlin, Rose invented a perfumed type of paper which was burned much like incense to dispel household odors. She also ran a perfumery in New York City for the first few years after her arrival in America.

- Rose never charged admission fees to her speeches, nor did she collect contributions to pay for her travel and lecturing costs. Her husband financially supported her lifelong reform work through his business as a silversmith in New York City.

For Further Reading

Stanton, Elizabeth Cady, Susan B. Anthony, and Matilda Joslyn Gage, eds. *History of Woman Suffrage.* Vol. I. Originally published in 1881. Reprinted. New York: Arno Press, 1969.

Suhl, Yuri. *Ernestine L. Rose: Women's Rights Pioneer.* 2nd ed. New York: Biblio Press, 1990.

Women and Economics

Written by Charlotte Perkins Gilman
Published in 1898

Charlotte Perkins Gilman was born in 1860 on the eve of the American Civil War. As a writer and lecturer, she became the leading intellectual force in the women's rights movement during the early twentieth century. While her contemporaries focused their efforts on securing women's right to vote, Gilman examined women's rights from a broader context. Her classic work *Women and Economics* outlines her concerns and recommendations regarding women's economic role in society.

Gilman believed that by limiting women's role to homemaker and mother, society had made women completely dependent on men. True equality would only be gained when women became full economic partners with men by working outside of the home. Published in 1898, *Women and Economics* won Gilman widespread fame in America and Europe. The book was quickly translated into seven languages, including Japanese, Russian, and Hungarian. People around the world discussed her compelling and radical ideas concerning women and work.

A turn-of-the-century typist receives instructions from her male boss.

Gilman began her literary career in the early 1890s while living in California. After leaving New England when her first marriage failed, she supported herself and her only daughter by writing, tutoring, lecturing, and even running a boardinghouse. She received a degree of recognition with the publication of a small volume of poems called *In This Our World.* Her fame and influence continued to grow as she lectured and published essays discussing various political and social issues of the time. Gilman attended women's suffrage (the right to vote) meetings and traveled throughout the United States and England to give lectures during the late 1890s. In 1897 during a bout of severe depression—a condition she battled throughout her life—she sought relief by writing. Within 17 days she had completed the draft of what would become her most famous book, *Women and Economics.*

In her book Gilman examines the question of how women can achieve equality in an industrial society. Many of the recommendations she describes in *Women and Economics* have come to pass over the years. For example, the majority of American women in the late twentieth century are employed to help support themselves and their families. And dual-career families are coming close to realizing her concepts of day care and "kitchen-less homes." Gilman felt that both husbands and wives should pursue professional careers and rely on other professionals for the traditional homemaking duties such as child care and cooking. The following excerpt is but a small sample of one of the most important books in American social and intellectual history. As a contributor to the magazine *Nation* remarked in June 1899, Gilman's book is "the most significant utterance on the subject [of women] since [John Stuart] Mill's [see entry] *Subjection of Women.*"

Things to Remember While Reading the Selection from
Women and Economics:

• Notice the influence of Charles Darwin, the naturalist who wrote *The Origin of Species by Means of Natural Selection* in 1859. Gilman argues that just as in Darwin's animal kingdom, men and women evolve as conditions in society change over time.

• She observes that the women of her era were economically dependent on men. While society was at this time beginning to change, Gilman hoped her writing would speed up the process leading to increased economic independence for women.

• Gilman urges women to develop "economically" by learning how to support themselves financially. Society would be vastly improved for both sexes, she suggests, if women moved beyond the limiting and unpaid roles of mother and homemaker.

Women and Economics

PREFACE

This book is written to offer a simple and natural explanation of one of the most common and most perplexing problems of human life,—a problem which presents itself to almost every individual for practical solution, and which demands the most serious attention of the **moralist***, the physician, and the sociologist—*

To show how some of the worst evils under which we suffer, evils long supposed to be **inherent** *and* **ineradicable** *in our natures, are but the result of certain arbitrary conditions of our own adoption, and how, by removing those conditions, we may remove the evils resultant—*

To point out how far we have already gone in the path of improvement, and how irresistibly the social forces of to-day are

Moralist: *Teacher or student of morals.*

Inherent: *Essential; found naturally.*

Ineradicable: *Incapable of being eradicated or eliminated.*

compelling us further, even without our knowledge and against our violent opposition,—an advance which may be greatly quickened by our recognition and assistance—

*To reach … especial[ly] the thinking women of to-day, and urge upon them a new sense, not only of their social responsibility as individuals, but of their measureless **racial** importance as makers of men.*

It is hoped also that the theory advanced will prove sufficiently suggestive to give rise to such further study and discussions as shall prove its error or establish its truth.

[CHAPTER] I.

*SINCE we have learned to study the development of human life as we study the evolution of species throughout the animal kingdom, some peculiar phenomena which have puzzled the philosopher and moralist for so long, begin to show themselves in a new light. We begin to see that, so far from being **inscrutable** problems, requiring another life to explain, these sorrows and perplexities of our lives are but the natural results of natural causes, and that, as soon as we **ascertain** the causes, we can do much to remove them.*

In spite of the power of the individual will to struggle against conditions, to resist them for a while, and sometimes to overcome them, it remains true that the human creature is affected by his environment, as is every other living thing….

*Attention is now called to a certain marked and peculiar economic condition affecting the human race, and unparalleled in the **organic** world. We are the only animal species in which the female depends on the male for food, the only animal species in which the sex-relation is also an economic relation. With us an entire sex lives in a relation of economic dependence upon the other sex, and the economic relation is combined with the sex-relation. The economic status of the human female is relative to the sex-relation….*

In studying the economic position of the sexes collectively, the difference is most marked. As a social animal, the

Racial: Relating to a particular group (in this case, not in terms of race as known in modern terms).

Inscrutable: Difficult to understand.

Ascertain: To determine by examination.

Organic: Living organisms.

Women's Contribution to a War a World Away

The outbreak of World War II forced the American economy out of the Great Depression (a period of severe economic crisis in the 1930s) and brought about unprecedented industrial growth. While the armed forces needed large numbers of young and middle-aged men, factories and industries needed replacement workers during the war to produce supplies for the growing army. Industry turned to an untapped labor source and began recruiting women for work in nontraditional roles, including machinists, welders, riveters, and fabricators.

During the war many women volunteered to join the armed forces. While regulations prevented them from serving in combat situations, the army directed women to serve in many other roles within the armed forces. The Women's Army Corps (WACS) performed noncombat functions for the army, including clerking, managing supply efforts, and pro-viding health care and food service. WAC members received benefits similar to their male counterparts, including insurance and health care. After the war they were also eligible for the benefits provided by the new G.I. Bill, which helped veterans attend college and purchase homes.

More than 25,000 women applied to join the Women's Army Service Pilots (WASPS) organization. From this large pool of applicants, two thousand were selected to participate in the rigorous Army Air Corps flight training program. Those who passed flew the same high performance fighters and heavy bombers as men but did not participate in combat. Instead, the women pilots flew newly constructed planes from the factories to the bases where combat crews were training. They also towed targets, tested aircraft, ferried planes overseas to replace planes lost in combat, and performed other duties to free men for combat roles.

economic status of man rests on the combined and exchanged services of vast numbers of progressively specialized individuals. The economic progress of the race, its maintenance at any period, its continued advance, involve the collective activities of all the trades, crafts, arts, manufactures, inventions, discoveries, and all the civil and military institutions that go to maintain them. The economic status of any race at any time, with its involved effect on all the **constituent** individuals,

Constituent: Member of a group; an essential part or element.

Many women—like these newly-graduated B-17 pilots—were trained to perform traditionally "male" tasks during World War II.

depends on their world-wide labors and their free exchange. Economic progress, however, is almost exclusively masculine. Such economic processes as women have been allowed to exercise are of the earliest and most primitive kind. Were men to perform no economic services save such as are still performed by women, our racial status in economics would be reduced to most painful limitations.

To take from any community its male workers would paralyze it economically to a far greater degree than to remove its female workers. The labor now performed by the women could be performed by the men, requiring only the setting back of many advanced workers into earlier forms of industry; but the labor now performed by the men could not be performed by the women without generations of effort and adaptation. Men can cook, clean, and sew as well as women; but the making and managing of the great engines of modern *industry, the threading of earth and sea in our vast systems of transportation, the handling of our elaborate machinery of trade, commerce, government,—these things could not be done so well by women in their present degree of economic development.*

*This is not owing to lack of the essential human **faculties** necessary to such achievements, nor to any inherent **disability** of sex, but to the present condition of woman, forbidding the development of this degree of economic ability. The male human being is thousands of years in advance of the female in economic status. Speaking collectively, men produce and distribute wealth; and women receive it at their hands. As men hunt, fish, keep cattle, or raise corn, so do women eat game, fish, beef, or corn. As men go down to the sea in ships, and bring coffee and spices and silks and gems from far away, so do women partake of the coffee and spices and silks and gems the men bring.*

The economic status of the human race in any nation, at any time, is governed mainly by the activities of the male: the female obtains her share in the racial advance only through him.

*Studied individually, the facts are even more plainly visible, more open and familiar. From the day laborer to the millionnaire, the wife's worn dress or flashing jewels, her low roof or her lordly one, her weary feet or her rich **equipage**— these speak of the economic ability of the husband. The comfort, the luxury, the necessities of life itself, which the woman receives, are obtained by the husband, and given her by him. And, when the woman, left alone with no man to "support" her, tries to meet her own economic necessities, the difficulties which confront her prove conclusively what the general economic status of the woman is. None can deny these **patent** facts,—that the economic status of women generally depends upon that of men generally, and that the economic status of women individually depends upon that of men individually, those men to whom they are related....*

Faculties: *Abilities or powers.*
Disability: *Incapacity.*
Equipage: *Horse-drawn carriage.*
Patent: *Obvious.*

Property and Labor | 201

The working power of the mother has always been a prominent factor in human life. She is the worker par excellence, *but her work is not such as to affect her economic status. Her living, all that she gets,—food, clothing,* **ornaments**, *amusements, luxuries,—these bear no relation to her power to produce wealth, to her services in the house, or to her motherhood. These things bear relation only to the man she marries, the man she depends on,—to how much he has and how much he is willing to give her. The women whose splendid extravagance dazzles the world, whose economic goods are the greatest, are often neither houseworkers nor mothers, but simply the women who hold most power over the men who have the most money. The female of genus homo is economically dependent on the male. He is her food supply. (Gilman, pp. xxix, 1-22)*

What happened next...

The success of *Women and Economics* secured Gilman's own economic well being. With her newfound financial freedom she began publishing her own monthly magazine, *The Forerunner,* in 1909. Gilman wrote practically every word that appeared in the magazine, including the few advertisements she accepted. She also serialized several of her novels, including her most famous utopian (depicting the search for and attainment of a perfect society) novel, 1915's *Herland,* which dramatizes some of her ideas concerning the roles of men and women in society.

Gilman helped shaped an entire era in American history as women sought to achieve greater rights. By urging women and men to assume responsibility for their own development, she helped open new opportunities for both sexes. As with other activists, Gilman's popularity diminished with the passage of the Nineteenth Amendment (guaranteeing women's suffrage) in 1920.

Ornaments: Accessories.

Charlotte Perkins Gilman

Charlotte Perkins Gilman (1860-1935) was born in Hartford, Connecticut, just prior to the outbreak of the Civil War; her father abandoned his wife and children shortly after her birth. Consequently, Gilman, her brother, and her mother were forced to move 19 times in 18 years to 14 different cities as they sought employment and charity from friends and family. Gilman learned to read before she was five but received only brief formal education at the Rhode Island School of Design. This training enabled her to contribute to the family's income by working as an art teacher and a governess, as well as a commercial artist designing greeting cards.

Did you know...

- Gilman is the grandniece of three famous American siblings: Catherine Beecher, early supporter of women's education; Harriet Beecher Stowe, author of the antislavery novel *Uncle Tom's Cabin;* and Henry Ward Beecher, preacher and abolitionist.

- Gilman did not consider herself a "feminist" but rather saw herself as a "sociologist." Sociology, which attempts to explain collective human behavior, was a relatively new social science in Gilman's era.

- Her best fictional work, *The Yellow Wall-Paper,* was first published in 1892. Still popular today, this haunting autobiographical short story describes the desolation of domestic life and a young wife's descent into madness.

- Ill with breast cancer, Gilman committed suicide when she was 75 years old in 1935. The note she left behind to her daughter explained that she "preferred chloroform to cancer."

For Further Reading

Gilman, Charlotte Perkins. *Women and Economics.* Originally published in 1898. Reprinted. New York: Harper TorchBooks, 1966.

Hill, Mary A. *Charlotte Perkins Gilman: The Making of a Radical Feminist, 1860-1896.* Philadelphia: Temple University Press, 1980.

Lane, Ann J. *To Herland and Beyond: The Life and Works of Charlotte Perkins.* New York: Pantheon Books, 1990.

Nation, June 1899.

First Days at Hull-House

A selection from Twenty Years at Hull-House
Written by Jane Addams
Published in 1910

In 1881, when she was 21 years old, Jane Addams experienced two tragedies that changed her life forever. She was devastated by the death of her father, an idealist with Quaker beliefs who had been an Illinois state senator for 16 years. In addition, she faced heartbreaking turmoil when illness forced her to end her medical school studies. Addams underwent an operation in the hopes that it would alleviate her condition; instead, the surgery left her unable to walk for two years. Fighting depression and feeling lost about what to do with her life, she took two long trips to Europe between 1883 and 1888. Addams found the inspiration she had been searching for during her second trip, when she and her friend Ellen Gates Starr visited London.

The two young women toured a "settlement house" called Toynbee Hall, which was an experimental project involving young men who planned to enter the ministry. These well-educated men moved into a poverty-ridden section of London and provided literacy classes and other activities for the poor. Since the men settled into the neighborhood and did not just visit, they called their

Addams and her friend Ellen Gates Starr built Hull House in one of Chicago's poorest slums.

headquarters a settlement house. Addams saw the potential of developing a similar project to help America's urban poor and provide an enriching experience for young middle-class women. She knew firsthand well-educated American women would appreciate the opportunity to "learn of life from life itself."

In September 1889 Addams and Starr moved into a large old mansion in one of Chicago's poorest slums. They began to help the underprivileged immigrants in the area by offering various forms of assistance. At first they provided a kindergarten, then quickly added a day nursery so mothers could safely leave their children while they worked. They expanded classes to teach English, as well as civic, cultural, recreational, and educational topics. While the young people who came to live in Hull-House helped introduce immigrants to American life, they themselves learned about life in other countries from their students.

Addams and other residents also lobbied for legislation that would improve the lives of their immigrant neighbors. The

Hull-House activists had many triumphs, including passage of the Factory Inspection Act, the establishment of the first juvenile court, child labor reform, and tenement housing regulations. They also helped end sweatshop working conditions, created better public parks and playgrounds, organized labor unions, and worked for international peace.

The success of Hull-House won international praise. Addams's experiment to humanize an industrial city attracted visitors from all over the world. By 1910 more than four hundred settlement houses existed across the country. Thousands of young women volunteered at these community centers helping immigrants adjust to their new homes in America.

Things to Remember While Reading
"First Days at Hull-House":

• Addams and Starr began their settlement experiment in 1889 with a single building, an old mansion built by Charles J. Hull. Their success over the next 20 years enabled them to construct a dozen more buildings by 1910.

• Addams talks about the challenges facing immigrants, including prejudice and discrimination, the stigma of being poor, and the living conditions in slum areas. By bringing people together from different economic and social backgrounds, she strove to end the isolation and poverty of immigrants.

• She refers to Canon Samuel A. Barnett, founder of the Toynbee Hall settlement project in London. Addams shares his hope for improving social relations since "the things which make men alike are finer and better than the things that keep them apart."

First Days at Hull-House

THE next January found Miss Starr and myself in Chicago, searching for a neighborhood in which we might put our plans into execution. In our eagerness to win friends for the new undertaking, we utilized every opportunity to set forth the meaning of the settlement as it had been embodied in [London's] Toynbee Hall, although in those days we made no appeal for money, meaning to start with our own slender resources. From the very first the plan received courteous attention, and the discussion, while often skeptical, was always friendly....

Three weeks later, with the advice of several of the oldest residents of Chicago ... we decided upon a location somewhere near the junction of Blue Island Avenue, Halsted Street, and Harrison Street. I was surprised and overjoyed on the very first day of our search for quarters to come upon the **hospitable** old house.... The house was of course rented, the lower part of it used for offices and storerooms in connection with a factory that stood back of it. However, after some difficulties were overcome, it proved to be possible to sublet the second floor and what had been the large drawing-room on the first floor.

The house had passed through many changes since it had been built in 1856 for the homestead of one of Chicago's pioneer citizens, Mr. Charles J. Hull, and although battered by its **vicissitudes**, was essentially sound. Before it had been occupied by the factory, it had sheltered a second-hand furniture store, and at one time the Little Sisters of the Poor had used it for a home for the aged. It had a half-skeptical reputation for a haunted attic, so far respected by the tenants living on the second floor that they always kept a large pitcher full of water on the attic stairs. Their explanation of this custom was so incoherent that I was sure it was a survival of the belief that a ghost could not cross running water, but perhaps that interpretation was only my eagerness for finding folklore.

The fine old house responded kindly to repairs, its wide hall and open fireplaces always insuring it a gracious aspect. Its generous owner, Miss Helen Culver, in the following spring gave us a free leasehold of the entire house. Her kindness has continued through the years until the group of thirteen buildings, which at present comprises our equipment, is built largely upon land which Miss Culver has put at the service of

Hospitable: Welcoming to guests.
Vicissitudes: Changes.

Addams

Jane Addams

Jane Addams (1860-1935) was born in Cedarville, Illinois. She was only two years old when her mother died. Consequently, Addams became very attached to her father and felt that their relationship profoundly influenced her life. In 1881 she graduated from the Rockford Female Seminary in Illinois as valedictorian and president of her class. Later, coping with her own illness and grief over her father's death, she spent several years unsure of what to do with her life. Besides settlement work, Addams was active in pacifism and the women's suffrage (right to vote) movement. She wrote hundreds of articles and several books, including her most famous, *Twenty Years at Hull-House*.

the Settlement which bears Mr. Hull's name. In those days the house stood between an **undertaking** establishment and a saloon. "Knight, Death, and the Devil," the three were called by a Chicago wit, and yet any mock heroics which might be implied by comparing the Settlement to a knight quickly dropped away under the genuine kindness and hearty welcome extended to us by the families living up and down the street.

We furnished the house as we would have furnished it were it in another part of the city, with the photographs and other **impedimenta** we had collected in Europe, and with a few bits of family mahogany. While all the new furniture which was bought was enduring in quality, we were careful to keep it in character with the fine old residence. Probably no young matron ever placed her own things in her own house with

Undertaking: The business of arranging funerals, cremations, and burials.

Impedimenta: Objects that impede or get in the way.

more pleasure than that with which we first furnished Hull-House. We believed that the Settlement may logically bring to its aid all those **adjuncts** which the cultivated man regards as good and suggestive of the best life of the past.

On the 18th of September, 1889, Miss Starr and I moved into it ... [and in] our enthusiasm over "settling," the first night we forgot not only to lock but to close a side door opening on Polk Street, and were much pleased in the morning to find that we possessed a fine illustration of the honesty and kindliness of our new neighbors.

Our first guest was an interesting young woman who lived in a neighboring tenement, whose widowed mother aided her in the support of the family by scrubbing a downtown theater every night. The mother, of English birth, was well bred and carefully educated, but was in the midst of that bitter struggle which awaits so many strangers in American cities who find that their social position tends to be measured solely by the standards of living they are able to maintain. Our guest has long since married the struggling young lawyer to whom she was then engaged, and he is now leading his profession in an eastern city. She recalls that month's experience always with a sense of amusement over the fact that the succession of visitors who came to see the new Settlement invariably questioned her ... concerning "these people" without once suspecting that they were talking to one who had been identified with the neighborhood from childhood. I at least was able to draw a lesson from the incident, and I never addressed a Chicago audience on the subject of the Settlement and its vicinity without inviting a neighbor to go with me, that I might curb any hasty generalization by the consciousness that I had an auditor who knew the conditions more intimately than I could hope to do....

Volunteers to the new undertaking came quickly; a charming young girl conducted a kindergarten in the drawing-room, coming regularly every morning from her home in a distant part of the North Side of the city. Although a **tablet** to her memory has stood upon a mantel shelf in Hull-House for five years, we still associate her most vividly with the play of little children, first in her kindergarten and then in her own nursery, which furnished a **veritable** illustration of Victor Hugo's [famous nineteenth-century French author known for his social and historical commentary] definition of heaven,—"a place where parents are always young and children always little." Her daily presence for the first two years made it quite impossible for us to become too solemn and self-conscious in our strenuous routine, for her **mirth** and **buoyancy** were irresistible and her eager desire to share the life of the neighborhood never failed, though it was often put to a severe test....

That first kindergarten was a constant source of education to us. We were much surprised to find social distinctions even among its **lambs,** although greatly amused with the neat formulation made by the superior little Italian boy who refused to sit beside **uncouth** little Angelina because "we eat our macaroni this way,"—imitating the movement of a fork from a plate to his mouth,— "and she eat her macaroni this way," holding his hand high in the air and throwing back his head, that his wide-open mouth might receive an imaginary cascade. Angelina gravely nodded her little head in approval of this distinction between gentry and peasant. "But isn't it astonishing that merely table manners are made such a test all the way along?" was the comment of their democratic teacher....

We were also early impressed with the curious isolation of many of the immigrants; an Italian woman once expressed her pleasure in the red roses that she saw at one of our receptions in surprise that they had been "brought so fresh all the way from Italy." She would not believe for an instant that they had been grown in America. She said that she had lived in Chicago for six years and had never seen any roses, whereas in Italy she had seen them every summer in great **profusion.** During all that time [in Chicago], ... the woman had lived within ten blocks of a florist's window; she had not been more than a five-cent car ride away from the public parks; but she had never dreamed of faring forth for herself, and no one

Veritable: *Real, true, or authentic.*

Mirth: *Gladness, especially expressed with laughter.*

Buoyancy: *Cheerfulness.*

Lambs: *Children.*

Uncouth: *Ungraceful, unrefined.*

Profusion: *Abundance.*

had taken her. Her conception of America had been the untidy street in which she lived and had made her long struggle to adapt herself to American ways.

But in spite of some untoward experiences, we were constantly impressed with the uniform kindness and courtesy we received. Perhaps these first days laid the simple human foundations which are certainly essential for continuous living among the poor: first, genuine preference for residence in an industrial quarter to any other part of the city, because it is interesting and makes the human appeal; and second, the conviction, in the words of Canon Barnett, that the things which make men alike are finer and better than the things that keep them apart, and that these basic likenesses, if they are properly **accentuated,** *easily transcend the less essential differences of race, language, creed and tradition.*

Perhaps even in those first days we made a beginning toward that object which was afterwards stated in our charter: "To provide a center for a higher civic and social life; to institute and maintain educational and **philanthropic** *enterprises, and to ... improve the conditions in the industrial districts of Chicago." (Addams, pp. 89-112)*

What happened next...

Addams became very involved in the international peace movement when World War I broke out in 1914. As a pacifist, or person opposed to war, she felt strongly about the need to settle conflicts through mediation. In 1915 she served as chair of the Women's Peace Party and the International Congress of Women, which met at The Hague in the Netherlands. The same year she helped establish the Women's International League for Peace and Freedom, serving as president from 1915 to 1929. Addams traveled to Europe often to attend peace conferences and meet with international leaders. When the United States entered the

Accentuate: To emphasize.
Philanthropy: Effort to increase well-being of humankind.

war in 1917, many Americans criticized her continued pacifist activities. However, in 1931 she was awarded the Nobel Peace Prize along with Nicholas Murray Butler, an educator and pacifist. In a true humanitarian gesture, Addams donated her share of prize money to the Women's International League for Peace and Freedom. She continued to work for the interests of the poor until her death in 1935.

Did you know...

- Addams was born into a wealthy family and did not always realize that others were less fortunate than she was. In her autobiography she recalls her decision at age seven to one day have a large house near the small houses where poor people lived.

- The Chicago campus of the University of Illinois expanded into the Hull-House neighborhood in 1963. Today the original mansion still exists and serves as a museum dedicated to Jane Addams and the settlement experience.

- The Hull-House Association continues to operate several community centers in Chicago, providing child care, counseling, and housing.

For Further Reading

Addams, Jane. *Twenty Years at Hull-House*. Originally published in 1910. Reprinted. New York: Macmillan, 1968.

Kent, Deborah. *Jane Addams and Hull-House*. Chicago: Childrens Press, 1992.

McPherson, Stephanie Sammartino. *Peace and Bread: The Story of Jane Addams*. Minneapolis: Carolrhoda Books, 1993.

Milestones

A selection from The Autobiography of Eleanor Roosevelt
Published in 1961

Eleanor Roosevelt, one the most influential women of the mid-twentieth century, was a compassionate leader and devoted humanitarian. A niece of President Theodore Roosevelt, she grew up in a prominent New York City family involved with political and social causes. She began her career in public service in the early 1900s, shortly after returning from London where she had attended private school. Roosevelt volunteered for several social reform organizations, including the National Consumer's League, a women's group working to establish legislation that would protect working children and women. In 1905 she married her distant cousin, Franklin Delano Roosevelt (FDR), another Roosevelt destined to become a popular and controversial leader. FDR served as assistant secretary of the navy during World War I, as governor of New York State between 1928 and 1932, and as president of the United States from 1933 to 1945.

Decades after her death Eleanor Roosevelt is still remembered for her commitment to improving the lives of others. She contributed significantly to the development of national policies concerning the rights of African Americans and women. Her 12 years (1933-45) as first lady began with the Great Depression-era of the 1930s and ended shortly before the conclusion of World War II. She played an influential role in the New Deal, a wide-ranging federal program designed to bring about the nation's economic recovery from the depression. Roosevelt ensured that portions of the New Deal, such as work relief programs, were designated for women, African Americans, and youth. In fact, her belief in equality and civil rights for American blacks generated a great amount of criticism in her time.

Perhaps the most publicized demonstration of Roosevelt's support for black equality occurred in 1939. The influential Daughters of the American Revolution (DAR) practiced blatant racist policy by refusing to allow the famous and now-

Roosevelt in March, 1933.

legendary African American singer Marian Anderson to perform at Constitution Hall in Washington, D.C. After announcing her resignation from the DAR in her widely read newspaper column "My Day," Roosevelt helped arrange Anderson's concert at the Lincoln Memorial. A crowd of 75,000 people attended the singer's performance on Easter Sunday, 1939. The National Association for the Advancement of Colored People (NAACP) acknowledged Roosevelt by inviting her to present its prestigious Spingarn Medal to Anderson later that same year.

After FDR's death in 1945, President Harry S Truman appointed Roosevelt to be a U.S. delegate to the United Nations (UN). As chair of the UN Commission on Human Rights (1946-51), she played a fundamental role in the drafting and adoption of the Universal Declaration of Human Rights in 1948. Her work to ensure human rights is considered one of her most lasting contributions.

- On her seventy-fifth birthday, Roosevelt gives an inspirational account of her transformation from "an ugly duckling" to a great leader interested in global issues.

- Roosevelt and her husband traveled to Europe immediately after World War I, a conflict also known as the "Great War." The devastation she witnessed during her trip led to a lifelong commitment to world peace.

- Her willingness to champion many causes, including civil rights for blacks, made Roosevelt a target of criticism. She talks about the courage needed to continue working for one's goals despite people's disapproval.

Milestones

IN OCTOBER of 1959 I reached my seventy-fifth birthday. It was a busy day, as most of mine are, with little time for introspection. Nonetheless, it was, in a way, a milestone, and I found myself looking back along the way I had come, trying to get a long-range view of the journey I had made and, if I could, to evaluate it. I wanted, if possible, to draw a kind of **balance sheet,** *to formulate for myself the objectives I had and to estimate how far I had achieved them.*

This kind of introspection is one in which I rarely indulge. At times, of course, it is valuable in throwing light into dark places, but its danger is that one may easily tend to become self-absorbed in one's voyage of discovery and self-analysis.

People still ask me frequently how I planned my career and what over-all objective I had in mind. Actually I never planned a career, and what basic objective I had, for many years, was to grasp every opportunity to live and experience life as deeply, as fully, and as widely as I possibly could. It

Balance sheet: A summary of assets and debts of a business or individual.

seemed to me stupid to have the gift of life and not use it to the utmost of one's ability.

*I was not a gifted person but I was always deeply interested in every **manifestation** of life, good or bad. I never let slip an opportunity to increase my knowledge of people and conditions. Everything was **grist to my mill:** not only the things I saw but the people I met. Indeed, I could not express adequately the debt I owe to the friends who taught me so much about the world I live in. I had really only three assets: I was keenly interested, I accepted every challenge and every opportunity to learn more, and I had great energy and self-discipline.*

As a result, I have never had to look for interests to fill my life. If you are interested, things come to you, they seem to gravitate your way without your lifting a hand. One thing leads to another and another, and as you gain in knowledge and in experience new opportunities open up before you....

I am sure that my objectives, during those early years at least, were constantly changing. In the beginning, because I felt, as only a young girl can feel it, all the pain of being an ugly duckling, I was not only timid, I was afraid. Afraid of almost everything, I think: of mice, of the dark, of imaginary dangers, of my own inadequacy. My chief objective, as a girl, was to do my duty. This had been drilled into me as far back as I could remember. Not my duty as I saw it, but my duty as laid down for me by other people. It never occurred to me to revolt. Anyhow, my one overwhelming need in those days was to be approved, to be loved, and I did whatever was required of me, hoping it would bring me nearer to the approval and love I so much wanted.

As a young woman, my sense of duty remained as strict and rigid as it had been when I was a girl, but it had changed its focus. My husband and my children became the center of my life and their needs were my new duty. I am afraid now that I approached this new obligation much as I had my childhood duties. I was still timid, still afraid of doing something

Manifestation: *Form.*

Grist to my mill: *Something that can be turned to one's advantage; "grist" is a type of grain.*

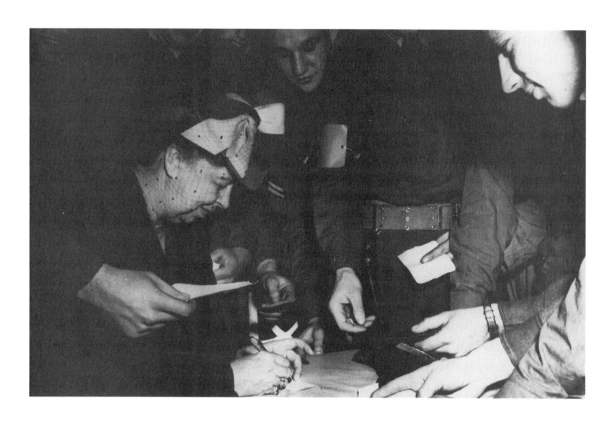

Roosevelt greets U.S.
Army Rangers during
a military exhibition.

wrong, of making mistakes, of not living up to the standards required by my mother-in-law, of failing to do what was expected of me.

As a result, I was so **hidebound** by duty that I became too critical, too much of a disciplinarian. I was so concerned with bringing up my children properly that I was not wise enough just to love them. Now, looking back, I think I would rather spoil a child a little and have more fun out of it.

It was not until I reached middle age that I had the courage to develop interests of my own, outside of my duties to my family. In the beginning, it seems to me now, I had no goal beyond the interests themselves, in learning about people and conditions and the world outside our own United States. Almost at once I began to discover that interest leads to interest, knowledge leads to more knowledge, the capacity for understanding grows with the effort to understand.

Hidebound: *Narrow-minded.*

From that time on, though I have had many problems, though I have known the grief and the loneliness that are the lot of most human beings, though I have had to make and still have to make endless adjustments, I have never been bored, never found the days long enough for the range of activities with which I wanted to fill them. And, having learned to stare down fear, I long ago reached the point where there is no living person whom I fear, and few challenges that I am not willing to face.

On that seventy-fifth birthday I knew that I had long since become aware of my over-all objective in life. It stemmed from those early impressions I had gathered when I saw war-torn Europe after World War I. I wanted, with all of my heart, a peaceful world. And I knew it could never be achieved on a lasting basis without greater understanding between peoples. It is to these ends that I have, in the main, devoted the past years.

One curious thing is that I have always seen life personally; that is, my interest or sympathy or indignation is not aroused by an abstract cause but by the plight of a single person whom I have seen with my own eyes. It was the sight of a child dying of hunger that made the tragedy of hunger become of such overriding importance to me. Out of my response to an individual develops an awareness of a problem to the community, then to the country, and finally to the world. In each case my feeling of obligation to do something has stemmed from one individual and then widened and become applied to a broader area.

More and more, I think, people are coming to realize that what affects an individual affects mankind. To take an extreme example, one neglected case of **smallpox** can infect a whole community. This is equally true of the maladjusted child, who may **wreak havoc** in his neighborhood; of the impoverished, who become either economic burdens or social burdens, and, in any case, are wasted as human beings. Abuses anywhere, however isolated they may appear, can end by becoming abuses everywhere....

Smallpox: *Highly infectious viral disease named for sores that leave pockmocks on the skin; the World Health Organization's smallpox vaccination program eradicated the disease globally.*

Wreak havoc: *To inflict widespread destruction.*

So I come to the larger objective, not mine, except as I am an American, but America's. It seems to me that America's objective today should be to try to make herself the best possible mirror of **democracy** that she can. The people of the world can see what happens here. They watch us to see what we are going to do and how well we can do it. We are giving them the only possible picture of democracy that we can: the picture as it works in actual practice. This is the only way other peoples can see for themselves how it works; and can determine for themselves whether this thing is good in itself, whether it is better than what they have, better than what other political and economic systems offer them....

We must, as a nation, begin to realize that we are the leaders of the **non-Communist** world, that our interests at some point all touch the interests of the world, and they must be examined in the context of the interests of the world. This is the price of leadership....

All this seems like a far cry from my seventy-fifth birthday and yet I find that, as I have grown older, my personal objectives have long since blended into my public objectives. I have, of course, realized that I cannot continue indefinitely the strenuous life I now lead, the constant traveling from state to state, country to country.

What, then? Then, I thought, even if I must relinquish much of my traveling, perhaps there is a way in which I can still reach people with things that it seems important for them to hear. The most practical way of doing this is through a radio or television program. My radio and television agent shook his head.

"You are too controversial a figure," he told me. "The sponsors would be afraid of you. Some of them feel so strongly about you that they believe the public would not buy any product on whose program you might appear."

I remembered then that some years earlier the head of the Red Cross had been afraid to accept a donation for fear that my participation would drive away other subscribers!

Democracy: Government by the people.

Non-Communist: Followers of a political, social, and economic order that promotes competition and free enterprise rather than state control of the production and distribution of goods.

Working Women's Rights Are Guaranteed by Law

The Equal Pay Act of 1963 is based directly on the findings of President John F. Kennedy's Commission on the Status of Women. Former First Lady Eleanor Roosevelt headed this commission, which was established in 1961. Despite Roosevelt's death in 1962 the commission completed its work and published the report *American Women* in October of 1963, only a month before the assassination of President Kennedy. The study outlined working women's greatest needs, including provisions for paid maternity leave and federal funding for child care centers. The Equal Pay Act of 1963 guaranteed "Equal pay for equal work" and became the first federal legislation ever to prohibit sex, or gender-related, discrimination.

The Civil Rights Act of 1964 assured all citizens of the United States freedom from discrimination based on race, color, religion, sex, or national origin. The Act established the federal Equal Employment Opportunity Commission (EEOC) to fight employment-related and on-the-job discrimination. In 1966 President Lyndon B. Johnson issued an executive order further solidifying the notion of equal employment opportunity. Large employers were encouraged to seek out minorities and women to fill positions as a good faith effort to correct past discriminatory practices. Businesses receiving federal funds or winning federal contracts were required to adopt programs that would recruit minorities and women to fill vacant positions. This executive order began the concept known as Affirmative Action.

The Civil Rights Act of 1991 specifically deals with sexual harassment on the job (persistent, annoying, and sometimes dangerous attacks—psychological or physical in nature—on a person because of her or his sex) and lists penalties for employers when harassment occurs. The 1991 act allows the courts to award compensation to victims and set punitive (punishing) damages against any employer when harassment has occurred.

It is startling to realize that one is so deeply, fanatically disliked by a number of people. And yet, while I weigh as honestly as I can their grounds for disapproval, when I feel that I am right in what I do, it seems to me that I cannot afford, as a self-respecting individual, to refuse to do a thing merely because

it will make me disliked or bring down a storm of criticism
on my head. I often feel that too many Americans today tend
to reject the thing, however right they believe it to be, that
they want to do because they fear they will be unpopular or will
find themselves standing alone instead of in the comfortable
anonymity of the herd.

As a result, when I believe, after weighing the evidence, that what I am doing is right I go ahead and try as hard as I can to dismiss from my mind the attitude of those who are hostile. I don't see how else one can live. (Roosevelt, pp. 410-16)

What happened next...

Roosevelt held her last major official position when President John F. Kennedy appointed her chair of his Commission on the Status of Women (CSW) in 1961. She died the following year of tuberculosis at the age of 78 before the group completed its work. As a tribute the commission issued its report, *American Women,* in 1963 on October 11—which would have been her seventy-ninth birthday. The CSW report recommended many policies, including the Equal Pay Act, which was enacted by Congress in 1963. This act became the first piece of legislation in U.S. history to prohibit discrimination based on sex and to require equal compensation for women and men who perform equal work.

Did you know...

• Roosevelt communicated with millions of Americans through her daily column "My Day," which appeared in 140 newspapers. She also wrote magazine articles and several books, appeared on radio talk shows, and traveled extensively on lecture tours. She donated all her earnings from these activities to charity.

• The first presidential wife to hold press conferences, Roosevelt established her own press corps of female reporters. By giving these women journalists "hard news" she helped forward their careers in the male-dominated world of newspaper reporting.

• Shortly after her husband's death in 1945 Roosevelt told reporters, "The story is over." However, she made some of her most important contributions during the next and final 17

Eleanor Roosevelt

Anna Eleanor Roosevelt (1884-1962) was born into the socially prominent Roosevelt family of New York. She was the niece of Theodore Roosevelt, who was president of the United States from 1901 to 1909. Roosevelt experienced a painfully lonely childhood and was raised by her grandmother after both her parents died. At the age of 15 she attended Allenswood, a private school in London. Roosevelt credits her headmistress, Marie Souvestre, with giving her the perspective that became the basis of her career in public service. In 1905 she married her distant constant, Franklin Delano Roosevelt (FDR), who would serve as president from 1933 to 1945, and together they had six children. She lived her life believing that "what one has to do usually can be done." Her accomplishments and humanitarian spirit continue to touch the lives of people around the world.

years of her life, particularly through her work as delegate to the United Nations.

- Eleanor and Franklin Roosevelt are buried in the rose garden of their home, Vall-Kill, in Hyde Park, New York, which today serves as a museum.

For Further Reading

Lash, Joseph. *Eleanor: The Years Alone.* New York: W. W. Norton, 1972.

Roosevelt, Anna Eleanor. *The Autobiography of Eleanor Roosevelt.* New York: Harper, 1961.

Civic and
Social Equality

Since the 1800s women have fought for recognition as the intellectual and social equals of men. Many women, such as feminist **Lucy Stone**, worked hard to gain their independence and to participate in public affairs. During the 1850s Stone was a popular speaker and leader of both the women's rights and abolition movements. As a single woman devoted to these important causes, she earned considerable income from her lectures and enjoyed the right to make her own business decisions. However, her decision to marry Henry Blackwell in 1855 meant the loss of both her legal independence and the right to control her own property. She and Blackwell declared their intentions to retain separate legal identities in a "marriage protest" that they published in many newspapers. Stone also pioneered the notion of a woman keeping her birth name after marriage rather than adopting the last name of her husband.

During the first half of the twentieth century **Alice Paul** worked hard to remind women that the right to vote was only one aspect of full equality. In 1923, on the seventy-fifth anniversary of the first women's rights convention in Seneca Falls, New York, Paul proposed the first **Equal Rights Amendment** (**ERA**). She lived to see the idea of equal rights incorporated into the charter of the United Nations and witnessed congressional passage of the ERA (although the amendment later died because of its failure to win state ratification).

One of the most famous authors of the twentieth century, **Virginia Woolf**, wrote poignantly about the discrimination women face in society. In her book *A Room of One's Own,* Woolf declared that in order for a woman to be a successful writer, she needed "five hundred [pounds; a form of British currency] a year and a room of one's own." Woolf believed women could realize great accomplishments only if they achieved economic independence and freedom from domestic responsibilities.

French philosopher **Simone de Beauvoir** researched the role of women in society for her book *The Second Sex.* She observed that society places less value on the roles of women than it does on the roles performed by men. According to de Beauvoir, women—the childbearers—have a lower status than men—the providers, conquerors, and inventors. Her radical assessments of gender stereotyping helped spark interest in the re-emerging women's rights movements in both America and Europe.

During the 1950s **Betty Friedan**, a freelancer, suburban housewife, and mother of three, published articles for various women's magazines, including the *Ladies' Home Journal.* However, she began to feel that something was missing from her life. Friedan went on to explore and relate the powerful effects of society's restrictive role for women in her bestselling 1963 book *The Feminine Mystique,* which helped start the "women's liberation" movement in America.

By 1966 a group of politically active women had founded the **National Organization for Women** (**NOW**). NOW aims to promote full equality for women and men in all aspects of society. The organization formed in response to the reluctance of the Equal Employment Opportunity Commission to enforce civil rights legislation that ensured women protection from employment discrimination. NOW played a significant role in convincing Congress to pass the ERA in 1972.

The women's liberation movement and the ERA were popular causes in the politically charged 1960s and 1970s. But strong opposition to the ERA soon developed. The organization Stop ERA fueled some women's fears that they would be drafted into the armed services and lose priority in child custody proceedings in the case of divorce. Stop ERA lobbied hard and has been given some credit for the eventual defeat of the ERA in 1982 (due to a lack of sufficient support at the state level).

In 1971 journalist and activist **Gloria Steinem** helped found *Ms.* magazine, the first exclusively female-controlled periodical. Instead of recipes and beauty columns typical of women's magazines, *Ms.* covers feminist issues and ideas. Despite their lack of funding, the publishers decided not to accept any advertising that portrayed women in an offensive way. Today, the magazine exists as an ad-free bimonthly financially supported by its subscribers. Steinem serves as a consulting editor and continues to give lectures, write books, and campaign for political candidates who support women's equality.

Selected correspondence, 1854–57

Written to and from Lucy Stone

Marriage of Lucy Stone under Protest, 1855

Written by Henry B. Blackwell and Lucy Stone

Lucy Stone pioneered the idea of women keeping their birth names after marriage. Before she met her husband, Henry B. Blackwell (often referred to as Harry in personal correspondence), Stone had already established herself as a successful orator, or public speaker. Shortly after her graduation from Oberlin College in 1847 at the age of 29, Stone began giving public lectures concerning women's rights and abolition, the movement to free slaves. She quickly became popular throughout the northeastern United States and received the nickname "Morning Star" as a leader of the emerging women's rights movement. Unlike many women of her day Stone supported herself from the fees she earned as a lecturer. In fact, she saved seven thousand dollars over three years, a considerable sum of money at the time.

When she fell in love with Henry Blackwell, Stone faced one of the most difficult decisions of her life—whether or not to risk losing her rights and her career by getting married. At the time married women had virtually no legal rights: they could not conduct their own business or even control their own income. Stone felt that marriage would result in the loss not just of her birth name but of the rights and reputation she had worked so hard to achieve. As a married woman she would be expected to stay at home and give up her public career as a reformer. Many of her opponents used to say they looked forward to the day when the "wedding kiss" would quiet her forever.

Blackwell, like Stone, believed in equality between the sexes and patiently courted her for five years as she hesitated about their future. Their wedding date of May 1, 1855, marked the beginning of one of the earliest egalitarian (equal partnership) marriages in American history. Stone created a great deal of controversy by deciding to keep her own name. In fact, the term "Lucy Stoner" became a popular phrase used when referring to single feminists or married women who decided to keep their birth names.

During their courtship and nearly 40 years of marriage Stone and Blackwell were frequently apart for long periods. Stone traveled extensively giving lectures and attending conventions in support of abolition and women's rights. Blackwell "stumped" (made political speeches) a great deal himself and traveled to the western territories on several occasions to conduct business. Living in an age without telephones, they kept in touch during their long journeys by writing letters to each other. The following excerpts are just a few samples of their several hundred surviving letters stored at the Library of Congress.

Things to Remember While Reading Stone's Selected Writings:

- Stone had deep reservations about marriage for many reasons, including the prospect of losing her identity and legal independence. As a married woman she would lose her right to conduct her own business affairs. At the beginning of their wedding ceremony Stone and Blackwell read aloud a "protest" about the unjust marriage laws that existed in the United States at the time.

- The anger expressed in Stone's letter to women's rights leader Susan B. Anthony reflects one of her worst fears about becoming married—that people would perceive her as being less committed to social reform than in her single days.

- As extensive letter writers Stone and Blackwell developed some interesting penmanship habits. Both tended not to use the apostrophe for contractions. For example, they spelled can't as "cant" and don't as "dont." Also the many words printed in italics below are actually words they had underlined for *emphasis*.

Letter to Lucy Stone from Henry B. Blackwell, 1854

Cincinnati December 22d 1854

My own dearest Lucy

... I ... travelled on horseback 45 miles over very rough roads, but on a beautiful day—crossed the Wabash [River] on a flat boat with my horse with some difficulty the ice running & rode 7 miles by Starlight over the prairie into town. There I recd [received] ... letters from various quarters & among them those two welcome ones from you.... My dear Lucy thank you a hundred times for all the strong, warm, beautiful love & confidence which fill & **animate** *those letters. I hope to show my thanks in something better than words in all the actions & feelings of my future life. Dear Lucy dont fear but that I will return you love for love to the fullest extent that your soul is capable of putting forth. You say that some one told you you had the capacity of love of 20 women. If so I will give you the love of as many men. I will* try *to be to you* all *that a man should* be *to the woman he loves—can I say more than that?*

In your last letter you tell me of the pain you experienced at the idea of being placed in the legal position of wife. I am very

Animate: *Bring to life.*

sorry *that you should thus suffer. But surely there is no* **degradation** *in being unjustly treated by others. The true degradation & disgrace rests not with the victim but with the oppressors.... After all what is the Law? It is nothing, unless appealed to.... It exists only where it is invoked. And even there, by taking proper steps we can anticipate & alter its possible action....*

Dear Lucy, we will live a pure & rational life. We will not be selfish, or impatient with each other in anything. We will advise together & each live out our own nature freely & frankly.... But Lucy dear—do not feel **constrained** *to marry me. Even now—or even on the very day itself, if you feel pain & shrinking postpone it just as long & as often as you please. Now you are my wife in sight of God by the divine tie of affection, I can wait as long as you please for its* **manifestation** *in this way. Dear Lucy you will break no faith & violate no compact if you leave me at any time either before, or after marriage. You are your own* **mistress** *& always will remain so. You speak of "Lucy Stone that was." You are the same Lucy that was & always will be. Dont feel badly on my a/c [account]. Dear Lucy—I would rather wait ten years & have no children than give you any unhappiness....*

As to your property dear—it will be necessary I suppose to settle all your personal property on yourself.... I do not know the law of Ohio, or Mass., but the best way will be to put it into the hands of trustees for your benefit.... Then we will engage to share earnings on both sides—you get half of mine & I half of yours, so long as we live together....

You shall choose when, where & how often you shall become a mother. Neither partner shall attempt to fix the residence, employment, or habits of the other—nor shall either partner feel bound to live together any longer than is agreeable to both.... For the sake of a good example we will draw up a contract specifying our course under all these various **contingencies** *of separation by* **dissention** *or death. But I feel & know so well that the first at least cannot happen, that it seems almost* **farcical** *for us so to specify.*

Degradation: *To lower in moral character; to disgrace.*

Constrained: *Forced.*

Manifestation: *Demonstration.*

Mistress: *A woman in a position of authority or control.*

Contingencies: *Events that may occur but most likely will not; alternate plans.*

Dissention: *Disagreement.*

Farcical: *Resembling a farce; absurd, silly.*

Lucy Stone

Lucy Stone (1818-1893) was born on her family's farm in West Brookfield, Massachusetts. Stone was the eighth of nine children. Her father believed in educating his sons but not his daughters, so she had to buy her own textbooks for primary school. She began teaching at the age of 16 to finance her advanced schooling. By 1843, when she was 25 years old, Stone had saved enough money to attend one semester at Oberlin College in Ohio. She struggled over the next fours years, working to pay for school expenses and managing to graduate in 1847. At Oberlin Stone became active in both the antislavery movement and issues concerning women's rights. She created considerable controversy by refusing to write her senior essay, since school policy forbade women from public speaking. Rather than have a male professor recite her essay at graduation, Stone led a protest of other students who also refused to write the required papers.

*Think over my suggestions on the previous pages.... I see no difficulty in the law for a loving marriage.... I like your idea of simple habits & a quiet mode of domestic life.... I have no relish for display. We shall find our happiness in comfort not show & in nobler things than costly **gewgaws**....*

Dear Lucy I must close my long letter. I want to meet you & take you into my arms again more than words can express.

Gewgaws:
Decorative trinkets.

God bless you & keep you my own little wife—& believe me ever yours

Harry
(Blackwell in Wheeler, pp. 108-11)

Marriage of Lucy Stone under Protest

It was my privilege to celebrate May day by officiating at a wedding in a farm-house among the hills of West Brookfield. The bridegroom was a man of tried worth, a leader in the Western Anti-Slavery Movement; and the bride was one whose fair name is known throughout the nation; one whose rare intellectual qualities are excelled by the private beauty of her heart and life.

I never perform the marriage ceremony without a renewed sense of the **iniquity** of our present system of laws in respect to marriage; a system by which "man and wife are one, and that one is the husband." It was with my hearty **concurrence,** therefore, that the following protest was read and signed, as a part of the nuptial ceremony; and I send it [so] that others may be **induced** to do likewise.

Rev. Thomas Wentworth Higginson

Protest.

While acknowledging our mutual affection by publicly assuming the relationship of husband and wife, yet in justice to ourselves and a great principle, we deem it a duty to declare that this act on our part implies no **sanction** of, nor promise of voluntary obedience to such of the present laws of marriage, as refuse to recognize the wife as an independent, rational being, while they confer upon the husband an injurious and unnatural superiority, investing him with legal powers which no

Iniquity: Injustice.
Concurrence: Agreement; cooperation; consent.
Induced: Led or moved
Sanction: Official approval or permission.

honorable man would exercise, and which no man should possess. We protest especially against the laws which give to the husband:

1. The custody of the wife's person.

2. The exclusive control and guardianship of their children.

3. The sole ownership of her personal, and use of her real estate, unless previously settled upon her, or placed in the hands of trustees, as in the case of minors, lunatics, and idiots.

4. The absolute right to the product of her industry.

5. Also against laws which give to the widower so much larger and more permanent an interest in the property of his deceased wife, than they give to the widow in that of the deceased husband.

6. Finally, against the whole system by which "the legal existence of the wife is suspended during marriage," so that in most States, she neither has a legal part in the choice of her residence, nor can she make a will, nor sue or be sued in her own name, nor inherit property.

We believe that personal independence and equal human rights can never be forfeited, except for crime; that marriage should be an equal and permanent partnership, and so recognized by law; that until it is so recognized, married partners should provide against the radical injustice of present laws, by every means in their power.

We believe that where domestic difficulties arise, no appeal should be made to legal **tribunals** under existing laws, but that all difficulties should be submitted to the equitable adjustment of **arbitrators** mutually chosen.

Tribunals: Courts of justice.
Arbitrators: People chosen to settle disputes.

Stone

Thus reverencing law, we enter our protest against rules and customs which are unworthy of the name, since they violate justice, the essence of all law.

Henry B. Blackwell,

Lucy Stone

(Stanton et al., pp. 260-61)

Letter to Susan B. Anthony from Lucy Stone, 1857

Orange, N.J. July 20, 1857

Dear Susan

I have waited for your second letter that I might answer them both in one.... [Stone discusses an upcoming women's rights convention that she cannot attend due to her pregnancy.]

Of course, you must use your own judgment about the time & place to discuss the marriage question. But when it is done, it seems to me, we must not call it, "woman's rights" for the simple reason, that it concerns men, just as much. Two days, & the previous evening will be none too much, for the good of the cause, provided you have speakers enough. I hope the convention will be all it ought to be, and I have no doubt it will. I shall try & send a letter.... [Stone then challenges Anthony's implication that Stone has reduced her women's rights activities since marrying Blackwell.]

My legal position as wife deprives me of the power to use a cent of all the money I have earned, or may earn, only as I get it through a third person. I cant sell legally what I have acquired without Harry's consent. If I sign any transfer of his property I am ever insulted by being "examined separately and apart from my husband" to know if it is by my own free will —my right to my name even is questioned and with all this smart, added to that I suffered as a woman, before I was a wife.

You were "terribly afraid" that in such **doting** ease, I should become nothing. O Susan, it was as wrong to you as to me. I cannot understand it.… I still believe that you are the same brave faithful worker, that I always have, and in my heart, are just as earnest blessings and **God speeds** for you, as ever—but I must make the path for my own feet. I have no advice or explanation to make to anybody.

With best wishes

Lucy

(Stone in Wheeler, pp. 170-71)

What happened next...

In the split that occurred within the women's rights movement after the Civil War, Lucy Stone help lead the faction supporting the Fourteenth and Fifteenth amendments, which granted voting rights to freed black male slaves but not to women—white or black. In 1869 she started the American Woman Suffrage Association (AWSA) and later established that organization's daily newspaper, the *Woman's Journal*. This publication became the longest running suffrage newspaper, lasting from 1870 to 1917. After Stone and Blackwell died, their daughter, Alice Stone Blackwell, continued serving as editor until 1917, when the *Journal* merged with two other suffrage papers to become the *Woman Citizen*.

Did you know...

• For several years Stone, like many other suffragists, wore *bloomers*—pants worn under a loose-fitting calf-length dress. She stopped wearing them, though, because controversy over her style of clothing seemed to be detracting from the cause of women's rights.

Doting: Showing excessive fondness.

God speed: Good fortune or luck; success.

- Blackwell tried to conserve paper for his letters by writing first horizontally and then vertically across the same page. After receiving one of his criss-crossed letters, Stone wrote back "I want to send you some money to buy paper with, so that you need dont *cross write* all your letters!!!"

- In 1893 at the age of 75 Lucy Stone died at her home in Dorchester, Massachusetts. On her deathbed Stone asked her daughter to try to "make the world better." Alice Stone Blackwell fulfilled her mother's request by working for many social causes during her life, including passage of the Nineteenth Amendment, which granted women the right to vote.

For Further Reading

Blackwell, Alice Stone. *Lucy Stone: Pioneer of Women's Rights.* Detroit: Grand River Books, 1971.

Hays, Elinor Rice. *Morning Star: A Biography of Lucy Stone, 1818-1893.* New York: Harcourt, Brace, 1961. Reprinted. New York: Octagon Books, 1978.

Kerr, Andrea Moore. *Lucy Stone: Speaking Out for Equality.* New Brunswick, New Jersey: Rutgers University Press, 1992.

Stanton, Elizabeth Cady, Susan B. Anthony, and Matilda Joslyn Gage, eds. *History of Woman Suffrage.* Vol. I. Originally published in 1881. Reprinted. New York: Arno Press, 1969.

Wheeler, Leslie, ed. *Loving Warriors: Selected Letters of Lucy Stone and Henry B. Blackwell, 1853 to 1893.* New York: Dial Press, 1981.

Selected writings 1921, 1924

All by Alice Paul

Women won the right to vote in 1920 with the final ratification of the Nineteenth Amendment. Many women who had worked for years to win suffrage—the right to vote—believed their battle was over. Other women, such as Alice Paul, viewed the Nineteenth Amendment as just the first step toward full equality. Some states, for example, still outlawed women from holding public office and from serving as jury members. Paul believed discrimination against women would end only with organized and sustained national opposition. As an experienced political leader, she felt a constitutional equal rights amendment would be the most efficient way to tackle widespread discrimination.

Paul played a major role in the final years of the suffrage struggle. In 1913 she focused efforts on a nationwide constitutional amendment when most other work was directed at the state level. Paul also introduced militant tactics such as parades, demonstrations, and hunger strikes—tactics she had learned from the British women's movement. She held a large parade of

Paul salutes suffrage with a grape juice toast, August 17, 1920.

more than five thousand suffragists the day before Woodrow Wilson's presidential inauguration in Washington, D.C., in 1913. Again Paul generated controversy when she continued to hold pickets in front of the White House despite the outbreak of World War I in 1917. After bystanders attacked the protesting women and destroyed their banners, the police arrested the women for "obstructing traffic."

Over the course of eight years Paul served as chair of the Congressional Union for Woman Suffrage, then chaired the National Woman's Party (NWP) from 1917 to 1921. With the passage of the Nineteenth Amendment, she became determined to maintain the momentum of women's organizations working toward equality. Her writings below include the editorial she wrote for the magazine the *Suffragist* and her opening remarks at the NWP convention in 1921.

Determined to help remove the remaining legal obstacles facing women, Paul proposed the first Equal Rights Amendment (ERA) in 1923. At a meeting in Seneca Falls on the 75th anniversary of the first women's rights convention, she read aloud the original Declaration of Sentiments written by Elizabeth Cady Stanton. Paul then introduced the amendment that she eventually named the "Lucretia Mott Amendment," in honor of one of the founders of the women's rights movement. As outlined in a 1924 NWP pamphlet, the ideas represented in the ERA clashed with the goals of most other women's organizations, which were working to establish "protective legislation" for women and children. These groups believed that working women needed legal protection to secure minimum wage and maximum hours.

Things to Remember While Reading
Paul's Selected Writings:

- Paul reminds members of the National Woman's Party (NWP) that suffrage was only one of the original resolutions discussed at the first women's rights convention held in Seneca Falls, New York, in 1848.

- Many women, including Paul, were physically and emotionally drained from their years of suffrage work. Paul implies that she will relinquish her leadership role within the NWP but expresses hope that the organization will continue its work.

- The 1923 NWP pamphlet argues against laws that ensure a minimum wage for working women. Other women's groups supported such "protective legislation," but the NWP opposed the precedent of treating women differently from men.

Editorial in the *Suffragist*
(January–February 1921)

WHEN the women of the United States first met to consider their position in the state and in human society, they drew up a Bill of Rights [a list of rights for women written by

Elizabeth Cady Stanton and based on the Declaration of Independence. Discussed and voted on at the first women's rights convention held in Seneca Falls, New York, in 1848] which—without power of any kind, political or economic, but with inspired determination—they started out to secure.

Almost seventy-three years from the date of that first convention, the women of the United States again meet to consider where they stand. During these seventy-three years, women have won the right without which all others are insecure, the right of a full and equal voice in the government under which they live.

Armed with this power, they meet now to consider the remaining forms of the subjection of women.

At that first convention in 1848, one of the resolutions unanimously adopted read:

"RESOLVED. That the women of this country ought to be enlightened in regard to the laws under which they live, that they may no longer publish their degradation by declaring themselves satisfied with their present position, nor their ignorance by asserting that they have all the rights they want."

This resolution still applies to the women of today. They have gained much since 1848, but they have made their gains piecemeal: rights which they possess in one state, they do not possess in another.

This, added to the fact that in many states laws are not coded, makes it very difficult to secure accurate information in regard to their legal status, but enough facts have been collected to prove that the "present position" is not "satisfactory."

Many of the laws against which the early convention protested continue to exist to the **detriment** and humiliation of women. Discriminations persist in the universities. Women are far from enjoying equality in the trades and professions. They are discriminated against by the Government itself in the Civil Service regulations. They do not share in all political

Detriment: *Injury, damage, or harm.*

offices, honors and **emoluments:** there is in one state at least a law which prevents women from holding office at all. They have not attained complete equality in marriage or equal rights as married women over their property or even in the matter of the guardianship of their children.

The very representation in Government which they have won in individual countries may lose its full significance by the creation of an international association of governments in which—unless they take prompt steps to secure it—they will not have an equal voice.

There is danger that because of a great victory women will believe their whole struggle for independence ended. They have still far to go. It is for the Woman's Party to decide whether there is any way in which it can serve in the struggle which lies ahead to remove the remaining forms of woman's subordination. (Paul in the Suffragist, January-February 1921)

Speech at the National Woman's Party Convention, February 16, 1921

We have called this convention together to close up the work connected with the suffrage campaign, and to turn over to you the question of the next step. The purpose for which this convention is assembled is an exceedingly serious one: to decide whether this organization which has battled for eight years for the political freedom of women shall, now that this object is obtained, disband, or whether it shall take up some other program and continue the battle along other lines. In the next three days the momentous decision is to be made whether the Woman's Party shall at the end of this week **furl** its banner forever, or whether it shall fling it forth on a new battle front.

This is probably the most important convention that the Woman's Party has ever held because of the seriousness of this decision to be made. We will report to you on the **discharge**

Emolument: Payment or compensation from employment.

Furl: To roll up.

Discharge: Fulfillment or performance.

Alice Paul

Alice Paul (1885-1977) was born in Moorsetown, New Jersey. She was one of four children of devout Quaker parents. (Quakers, members of the Christian sect known as the Society of Friends, lead lives of simplicity, tolerance, and peace.) After attending private schools, Paul graduated from Swarthmore College in 1905. She completed a social work fellowship and a master's degree in sociology before traveling to England in 1907 to attend a Quaker training school. While abroad she became involved with the militant suffrage tactics of Emmeline Pankhurst. Paul participated in demonstrations, served time in prison, and even took part in hunger strikes. Upon her return to the United States in 1910, she introduced an unswerving spirit into the stagnant suffrage movement. Besides the doctoral degree she earned from the University of Pennsylvania, Paul received several law degrees. She devoted her entire life to achieving equality for women.

of the responsibility which has been placed in our keeping with regard to the work which is just over. We will then ask representatives from all the existing national organizations of women, as many leading women from other countries as we have been able to assemble here, and representatives from all the existing national political parties, to tell you what their programs are, so that you may have a clear view of the whole situation when you make your decision as to whether it is wise for the Woman's Party to disband, and if not, upon what program it shall next concentrate.

Many of the members of our Committee feel that they cannot, now that the suffrage struggle is ended, take up immediately another strenuous campaign, but they are glad to turn over all machinery and connections which they have helped to build up, to any group in the organization which is willing to go forward with the effort to win complete freedom for women. We are all hopeful that some group will arise in this convention who will be ready to carry on the campaign for another stretch of the road leading to full freedom for women.

We, who are members of the National Executive Committee, feel a very deep gratitude to you who as officers and members in the various states have done so much to make possible the victory which we celebrated last night at the Capitol. We feel also a complete confidence, as a result of our wonderful eight years of comradeship with you, that the decision which you make this week will be one which will mean a better lot for women here and everywhere and for which generations of women to come will have reason to be grateful.

Into your hands we now place the conduct of this convention and the making of this decision.... (Paul in Party Papers: 1913-1974)

The Woman's Party and the Minimum Wage for Women, 1924

THE Woman's Party takes no stand upon minimum wage legislation, except that it stands for the principle that wage legislation, if enacted, should be upon a non-sex basis, as is already the case in various foreign countries.

The Woman's Party opposes a sex basis for a minimum wage law, because it believes that establishing minimum wage laws which apply to women but not to men, gives recognition

Equal Rights Amendment

Alice Paul first proposed the idea for a federal constitutional amendment for women's rights shortly after women were empowered at the ballot box. She introduced her draft of the ERA at a special convention held in July 1923 in Seneca Falls, New York—a site of historical importance, since the first women's rights convention took place there in 1848. Paul and other feminists dubbed the ERA the "Lucretia Mott Amendment" in honor of one of the founding leaders of the women's rights movement. The first ERA proposal introduced into Congress in 1923 stated simply: "Men and women shall have equal rights throughout the United States and every place subject to its jurisdiction. Congress shall have the power to enforce this article through appropriate legislation."

After decades of consideration, both houses of Congress passed the Equal Rights Amendment in 1972. Within one year 28 states ratified the ERA, which had been modified only slightly from the original 1923 version to read: "Equality of rights under the law shall not be denied or abridged by the United States or by any State on account of sex." By 1977 a total of 35 states had ratified the ERA. Final ratification required 38 states, leaving the ERA just three states short of becoming law. Congress granted a three-year extension for the ratification process in 1979; when it expired in 1982, however, the ERA was still three states short of final ratification.

to the idea that women are a class apart in industry who can only enter the industrial field by permission of the government and under various restrictions laid down by the government.

The Woman's Party contends that there is no more reason for a minimum wage law applying to women only, than for a minimum wage law applying to one particular race or one particularly creed.

That this point of view is gradually coming to be accepted is evidenced by the latest opinion of the United States Supreme Court on this subject. The Supreme Court, in discussing the minimum wage law for women in the District of Columbia, said in 1923:

*"We can not accept the doctrine that women of mature age, **sui juris,** require or may be subjected to restrictions upon their liberty of contract which could not lawfully be imposed in the case of men under similar circumstances. To do so would be to ignore all the implications to be drawn from the present-day trend of legislation, as well as that of common thought and usage, by which woman is accorded emancipation, from the old doctrine that she must be given special protection or be subjected to special restraint in her contractual and civil relationship."* (Adkins v. The Children's Hospital, 261, U.S. 525, 1923)

The courts are among the last places to reflect changes in popular opinion. When one finds the Supreme Court stating that women should be "accorded emancipation from the old doctrine that she must be given special [protection] or be subjected to special restraint in her contractual and civil relationship," one feels that the demand of the modern woman for Equal Rights with men in industry is at last beginning to be heard.

The modern woman wants "Equal Rights" with her male competitor in earning her living. She wants nothing more and nothing less. (Paul in Party Papers: 1913-1974))

What happened next...

When the original Equal Rights Amendment (ERA) failed to win congressional support in 1925, Paul realized the importance of gaining support from other women's organizations. The ERA directly challenged the protectionist measures (restrictions on competition or a guarantee of special treatment, in this case for women only) favored by the influential Women's Trade Union League and League of Women Voters. But a fresh wave of

Sui juris: Latin phrase meaning capable of taking care of one's own affairs.

legislation issued by President Franklin D. Roosevelt—collectively termed the New Deal—took hold in the 1930s, as the United States fought to recover from the widespread economic devastation of the Great Depression. New Deal labor initiatives overturned protective legislation by establishing maximum work hours and minimum wages for both women *and* men.

By the end of World War II in 1945, major women's organizations began to support the ERA. Paul helped write the final version of the ERA, which passed Congress in 1972. She died five years later, believing the amendment would receive the support of the final three states needed for ratification. But time ran out in 1982, with the ERA still short of the required 38 states.

Did you know...

- In 1917 Paul organized suffrage protests in front of the White House. Police arrested a total of 218 female picketers and sent 97 to jail for "obstructing traffic." Many jailed women, including Paul, went on hunger strikes to protest the treatment they received.

- While her family never publicly voiced their support, Paul did receive financial support from her widowed mother so she could devote herself full time to suffrage activities.

- Paul successfully lobbied to include the idea of sex equality in the preamble of the United Nations' charter.

For Further Reading

Lunardini, Christine A. *Suffrage to Equal Rights: Alice Paul and the National Woman's Party, 1910-1928.* New York: New York University Press, 1986.

National Woman's Party. *Party Papers: 1913-1974.* Glen Rock, New Jersey: Microfilming Corporation of America, 1978.

Suffragist, January-February 1921.

A Room of One's Own

*A selection from papers written by Virginia Woolf
Collected and published in 1929*

English novelist and essayist Virginia Woolf is considered one of the greatest experimental writers of the twentieth century. She is credited with redefining modern English literary style. Woolf mastered the "stream of consciousness" narrative technique, which James Joyce (the Irish author most famous for his classic novel *Ulysses*) and several other British writers also explored. Instead of presenting an organized, sequential plot, Woolf's stories peer into the minds of her characters, relating thoughts and actions as they occur. The author's beautifully crafted prose reflects a keen insight into human feelings and behaviors; passion, sexuality, alienation, despair, and the complexity of human relationships—especially those between men and women—are frequent topics in her writings.

In her 1929 essay *A Room of One's Own,* Woolf identifies the obstacles a female artist faces living in a male-dominated society. This highly personal narrative brings to life the consequences of lost human potential. Most of Woolf's works, including *A Room of One's Own,* remain popular even three-quarters of a century after their original publication.

Woolf was born Adeline Virginia Stephen in London, England, in 1882. As a young woman in her twenties she helped form an intellectual circle known as the Bloomsbury Group. After the deaths of her parents, which took a profound emotional toll on her, Stephen and her siblings had moved to a house in the Bloomsbury section of London. This modest home in Tavistock Square became a center of intellectual activity; Stephen hosted regular gatherings there that included her brother's friends from Cambridge University. The group boasted many leading intellectuals such as author E. M. Forster, economist John Maynard Keynes, and art critic Roger Fry.

In 1912 Stephen married Leonard Woolf, a fellow member of the Bloomsbury Group. Five years later the couple started their own publishing company, Hogarth Press. They began to publish the best and most innovative work by promising alternative writers. Over the years they printed many of Woolf's books and other important works, including *Prelude* by British short story writer Katherine Mansfield and *Poems* by T. S. Eliot, the highly influential American-born English writer who would later win the Nobel Prize for literature.

A Room of One's Own is based on two papers Woolf delivered at the women's colleges of Cambridge University. Published in 1929, the essay leads the reader through a wandering examination of the many challenges and obstacles women artists face in a male-centered society. Using her distinctive writing style and powers of observation, Woolf ponders the problem of gender-based inequity and speculates on the reasons why women have not written any great works like those, for instance, of sixteenth-century English poet and playwright William Shakespeare. Without the chance to receive an education and pursue a career, women in Woolf's time were unable to develop their natural talents. The author urges women of the future to forge ahead with their educations, their writing efforts, and their wildest dreams.

Things to Remember While Reading *A Room of One's Own*:

- Throughout her life Woolf was plagued by depression, anguish, and periods of mental collapse. She is said to have viewed the exhaustive process of writing both as a liberating source of self-exploration and release and as a laborious act that left her emotionally drained and, at times, nearly mad.

- Woolf is famous for her experimental writing style, which weaves her characters' innermost thoughts into a carefully constructed critique of human nature and society. In the sample provided below, notice how she sounds as if she is talking directly to the reader.

- To dramatize the difficulties women artists faced living in a male-dominated society in the early twentieth century, Woolf invents the character of Judith—the imaginary sister of Shakespeare. Judith symbolizes the wasted potential of women constrained by a backward society and left with few opportunities outside their traditional roles as daughters, wives, and mothers.

- According to Woolf women need two things in order to become successful writers: economic freedom and the autonomy to develop their craft. She poetically summarizes these two essentials as "five hundred [pounds] a year and a room of one's own." (Pounds are a form of British currency.)

A Room of One's Own

I could not help thinking, as I looked at the works of [William] Shakespeare on the shelf, that ... it would have been impossible, completely and entirely, for any woman to have written the plays of Shakespeare in the age of Shakespeare. Let me imagine, since facts are so hard to come by, what would have happened had Shakespeare had a wonderfully gifted sister, called Judith, let us say. Shakespeare himself went, very probably—his mother was an heiress—to the grammar school, where he may have learnt Latin—[literary classics by ancient poets] Ovid, Virgil and Horace—and the elements of grammar and logic. He was, it is well known, a wild boy who poached rabbits, perhaps shot a deer, and had, rather sooner than he should have done, to marry a woman in the neighbourhood, who bore him a child rather quicker than was right. That escapade sent him to seek his fortune in London. He had, it seemed, a taste for the theatre; he began by holding horses at the stage door. Very soon he got work in the theatre, became a successful actor, and lived at the hub of the universe, meeting everybody, knowing everybody, practising his art on the **boards,** exercising his wits in the streets, and even getting access to the palace of the queen. Meanwhile his extraordinarily gifted sister, let us suppose, remained at home. She was as adventurous, as imaginative, as **agog** to see the world as he was. But she was not sent to school. She had no chance of learning grammar and logic, let alone of reading Horace and Virgil. She picked up a book now and then, one of her brother's perhaps, and read a few pages. But then her parents came in and told her to mend the stockings or mind the stew and not **moon** about with books and papers. They would have spoken sharply but kindly, for they were substantial people who knew the conditions of life for a woman and loved their daughter—indeed, more likely than not she was the apple of her father's eye. Perhaps she scribbled some pages up in an apple loft on the sly, but was careful to hide them or set fire to them. Soon, however, before she was out of her teens, she was to be betrothed to the son of a neighbouring **wool-stapler.** She cried out that marriage was hateful to her, and for that she was severely beaten by her father. Then he ceased to scold her. He begged her instead not to hurt him, not to shame him in this matter of her marriage. He would give her a chain of beads or a fine petticoat, he said; and there were tears in his eyes. How could she disobey him? How could she break his heart? The force of her own gift alone drove her to it. She made up a small parcel of her belongings, let herself down by a rope one summer's night and took the road to

Boards: *A theater stage.*
Agog: *Highly excited.*
Moon: *To pass time aimlessly.*
Wool-stapler: *Dealer in wool.*

*London. She was not seventeen. The birds that sang in the hedge were not more musical than she was. She had the quickest fancy, a gift like her brother's, for the tune of words. Like him, she had a taste for the theatre. She stood at the stage door; she wanted to act, she said. Men laughed in her face. The manager—a fat, loose-lipped man—**guffawed**. He bellowed something about poodles dancing and women acting—no woman, he said, could possibly be an actress. He hinted—you can imagine what. She could get no training in her craft. Could she even seek her dinner in a tavern or roam the streets at midnight? Yet her genius was for fiction and lusted to feed abundantly upon the lives of men and women and the study of their ways. At last—for she was very young, oddly like Shakespeare the poet in her face, with the same grey eyes and rounded brows—at last Nick Greene the actor-manager took pity on her; she found herself with child by that gentleman and so—who shall measure the heat and violence of the poet's heart when caught and tangled in a woman's body?— killed herself one winter's night and lies buried at some crossroads where the omnibuses now stop outside the Elephant and Castle.*

That, more or less, is how the story would run, I think, if a woman in Shakespeare's day had had Shakespeare's genius.... Yet genius of a sort must have existed among women as it must have existed among the working classes. Now and again an Emily Brontë [the nineteenth-century British author of the tragic Wuthering Heights] *or a Robert Burns [the famous Scottish poet] blazes out and proves its presence. But certainly it never got itself on to paper. When, however, one reads of a witch being **ducked,** of a woman possessed by devils, of a wise woman selling herbs, or even of a very remarkable man who had a mother, then I think we are on the track of a lost novelist, a suppressed poet, of some mute and inglorious Jane Austen [the British novelist best known for* Sense *and* Sensibility *and* Pride *and* Prejudice]*, some Emily Brontë who dashed her brains out on the moor or mopped and*

Guffaw: A coarse burst of laughter.

Ducked: Suspected witches were ducked under water to see if they would float.

Virginia Woolf

Adeline Virginia Stephen (1882-1941)—best known by her married name, Virginia Woolf—was born in London, England, the third of four children. She grew up in a highly intellectual home where her father, Leslie Stephen, a prominent scholar and biographer, frequently entertained famous writers, poets, and philosophers. While one of her brothers attended Cambridge University, Woolf studied at home under her father's guidance. At age 13, in the painful aftermath of the death of her beloved mother, she suffered her first mental breakdown. Following her father's death less than a decade later, Woolf and her siblings moved to the Bloomsbury section of London, where they developed a circle of intellectual friends.

After her marriage to Leonard Woolf in 1912, the couple started Hogarth Press, a publishing company. Woolf achieved considerable recognition as a novelist and essayist and is still regarded as one of England's finest and most innovative writers. Of her many books, her best known are works of fiction, including *Mrs. Dalloway* (1925) and *To the Lighthouse* (1927). Plagued by bouts of mental illness throughout her life, Woolf committed suicide in 1941.

mowed about the highways crazed with the torture that her gift had put her to. Indeed, I would venture to guess that Anon, who wrote so many poems without signing them, was often a woman. It was a woman Edward Fitzgerald [an English poet and translator], I think, suggested who made the ballads and the folk-songs, crooning them to her children, **beguiling** her spinning with them, or the length of the winter's night.

This may be true or it may be false—who can say?—but what is true in it, so it seemed to me, reviewing the story of Shakespeare's sister as I had made it, is that any woman born with a great gift in the sixteenth century would certainly have gone crazed, shot herself, or ended her days in some lonely cottage outside the village, half witch, half wizard, feared and mocked at. For it needs little skill in psychology to be sure that a highly gifted girl who had tried to use her gift for poetry would have been so thwarted and hindered by other people, so tortured and pulled asunder by her own contrary instincts, that she must have lost her health and sanity to a certainty. No girl could have walked to London and stood at a stage door and forced her way into the presence of actor-managers…. To have lived a free life in London in the sixteenth century would have meant for a woman who was poet and playwright a nervous stress and dilemma which might well have killed her. Had she survived, whatever she had written would have been twisted and deformed…. And undoubtedly, I thought, looking at the shelf where there are no plays by women, her work would have gone **unsigned.** That refuge she would have sought certainly….

And one gathers from [the] enormous modern literature of confession and self-analysis that to write a work of genius is almost always a feat of **prodigious** difficulty. Everything is against the likelihood that it will come from the writer's mind whole and entire. Generally material circumstances are against it. Dogs will bark; people will interrupt; money must be made; health will break down. Further, accentuating all these difficulties and making them harder to bear is the world's notorious indif-

Beguiling: Passing time pleasantly.
Unsigned: Published as an anonymous work or under someone else's name (usually a man's).
Prodigious: Enormous.

ference. It does not ask people to write poems and novels and histories; it does not need them.... If anything comes through in spite of all this, it is a miracle, and probably no book is born entire and uncrippled as it was conceived.

But for women, I thought, looking at the empty shelves, these difficulties were infinitely more formidable. In the first place, to have a room of her own, let alone a quiet room or a sound-proof room, was out of the question, unless her parents were exceptionally rich or very noble, even up to the beginning of the nineteenth century. Since her **pin money,** which depended on the good will of her father, was only enough to keep her clothed, she was debarred from such alleviations as came even to [nineteenth-century English poets John] Keats or [Alfred, Lord] Tennyson or [nineteenth-century Scottish essayist and historian Thomas] Carlyle, all poor men, from a walking tour, a little journey to France, from the separate lodging which, even if it were miserable enough, sheltered them from the claims and tyrannies of their families. Such material difficulties were formidable; but much worse were the immaterial. The indifference of the world which Keats and [French author Gustave] Flaubert and other men of genius have found so hard to bear was in her case not indifference but hostility. The world did not say to her as it said to them, Write if you choose; it makes no difference to me. The world said with a guffaw, Write? What's the good of your writing?...

I told you in the course of this paper that Shakespeare had a sister; but do not look for her in Sir Sidney Lee's life of the poet. She died young—alas, she never wrote a word.... Now my belief is that this poet who never wrote a word and was buried at the crossroads still lives. She lives in you and in me, and in many other women who are not here tonight, for they are washing up the dishes and putting the children to bed. But she lives; for great poets do not die; they are continuing presences; they need only the opportunity to walk among us in the flesh. This opportunity, as I think, it is now coming within your power to give her. For my belief is that if we live another century or so—I am

Pin money: *Money given to housewives and daughters for incidental expenses.*

*talking of the common life which is the real life and not of the little separate lives which we live as individuals—and have **five hundred [pounds] a year** each of us and rooms of our own; if we have the habit of freedom and the courage to write exactly what we think; if we escape a little from the common sitting-room and see human beings not always in their relation to each other but in relation to reality; ... if we face the fact, for it is a fact, that there is no arm to cling to, but that we go alone and that our relation is to the world of reality and not only to the world of men and women, then the opportunity will come and the dead poet who was Shakespeare's sister will put on the body which she has so often laid down. Drawing her life from the lives of the unknown who were her forerunners, as her brother did before her, she will be born. As for her coming without that preparation, without that effort on our part, without that determination that when she is born again she shall find it possible to live and write her poetry, that we cannot expect, for that would be impossible. But I maintain that she would come if we worked for her, and that so to work, even in poverty and obscurity, is worth while. (Woolf, pp. 48-55, 117-118)*

What happened next...

Woolf devoted her life to writing and became obsessed by the fragmentation of society. Although she waged a valiant and ongoing battle against mental illness, in 1941—while experiencing the symptoms of what she feared would be a permanent mental breakdown—she drowned herself in the Ouse River in Sussex, England. She had written nearly 20 books before she died; another 20 volumes of essays, diaries, and letters were published posthumously (after her death). Woolf's entire body of work includes masterful examples of "stream of consciousness" writing and provides valuable insight into the author's own inner thoughts.

Five hundred [pounds] a year: According to Woolf, the amount of British currency needed to support oneself.

Did you know...

- The life and works of Virginia Woolf remain popular subjects for biographers and literary critics. Numerous scholarly books discuss her writing style and the interesting connections between her personal life and her fiction.

- Woolf was a witness to several wars, including World War I, the Spanish Civil War, and the outbreak of World War II. In her essay *Three Guineas* (1938), the author explores the relationship between war and a male-dominated society. She suggests that educated women in positions of power might be more capable than men at preventing war.

- In 1962 American playwright Edward Albee's sharp critique of American society, *Who's Afraid of Virginia Woolf?*, premiered on Broadway at the Billy Rose Theatre. This successful stage production, which was also adapted for film, follows a troubled intellectual couple through the decline of their marriage.

For Further Reading

Bell, Quentin. *Virginia Woolf: A Biography*. New York: Harcourt, 1972.

Daiches, David. *Virginia Woolf*. New Directions, 1963.

Gordon, Lyndall. *Virginia Woolf: A Writer's Life*. New York: Norton, 1984.

Rossi, Alice S., ed. *The Feminist Papers: From Adams to de Beauvoir*. New York: Columbia University Press, 1973.

Woolf, Virginia. *A Room of One's Own*. New York: Harcourt, 1929, reprinted, 1981.

Woolf, Virginia. *A Writer's Diary*. Edited by Leonard Woolf. New American Library, 1968.

The Second Sex

From the text written by Simone de Beauvoir
First published in French in 1949
Published in English translation in 1953

In 1946, as the accomplished French writer and philosopher Simone de Beauvoir began looking for ideas for her next book, she considered writing about what it meant to be a woman. Gradually she realized that many myths about the female gender had found their way into the fabric of Western culture. She became fascinated with these myths of femininity and the impact they have on women and society. After spending more than two years researching at the French national library, de Beauvoir completed her two-volume analysis of the subject, *Le Deuxième Sexe,* in 1949. This vast work of more than eight hundred pages was translated into English and published as *The Second Sex* in 1953.

While de Beauvoir based *The Second Sex* on her extensive study of anthropology, biology, psychology, sociology, literature, and history, she did not intend her work to be factual. She created what is termed a "polemical" book, meaning she wrote to present her argument against an established system of beliefs. Among her most radical ideas is the notion that innate, or natural,

feminine characteristics do not really exist. De Beauvoir suggests that Western culture teaches women and men to behave in certain ways. She states: "One is not born, but rather one becomes, a woman. No biological, psychological, or economic fate determines the figure that the human female presents in society; it is civilization as a whole that produces this creature ... which is described as feminine."

In *The Second Sex* de Beauvoir theorizes that men dominate society by deciding which roles are important and then assigning lesser value to the functions performed by women. For example, throughout history society has granted men considerable status and power as providers, inventors, and conquerors. But women, who are viewed mainly in terms of their role as childbearers, enjoy less status. The author offers harsh commentary on society's values: "In the human race," she writes, "superiority has been assigned not to the sex which gives birth but to the sex which kills."

de Beauvoir at a 1961 Paris news conference.

De Beauvoir stands as a symbol of clarity, logic, and reason in the murky waters of discrimination. Her book presents a powerful call for gender equity in all aspects of life. In spite of the biological differences between the sexes, she maintains that women should not be thought of merely as "the second sex."

De Beauvoir was genuinely surprised by the controversy generated by the publication of her feminist manifesto. Her alternative lifestyle and radical convictions, which sometimes seem extreme, brought her both worldwide fame and biting criticism.

Things to Remember While Reading *The Second Sex*:

- De Beauvoir examines the nature of femininity, offering her own thoughts on whether women are born with innate and natural characteristics or whether society teaches them to behave in certain ways. Her premise, "One is not born, but rather one becomes, a woman," sparked a new age of feminism throughout the world.

- She asserts that Western society regards men as the primary gender and women as secondary to them; women are defined most often in terms of their sexual relationship to men.

- De Beauvoir suggests that true equality and freedom for both sexes can only occur when females are viewed as an independent, separate, and equal gender. She urges women to take charge of their lives and establish identities that go beyond their dependent roles as daughters, wives, and mothers.

The Second Sex

For a long time I have hesitated to write a book on woman. The subject is irritating, especially to women; and it is not new. Enough ink has been spilled in the quarreling over feminism, now practically over, and perhaps we should say no more about it. It is still talked about, however, for the volumi-

nous nonsense uttered during the last century seems to have done little to illuminate the problem. After all, is there a problem? And if so, what is it? Are there women, really? Most assuredly the theory of the eternal feminine still has its adherents who will whisper in your ear: "Even in Russia women still are women"; and other **erudite** persons—sometimes the very same—say with a sigh: "Woman is losing her way, woman is lost." One wonders if women still exist, if they will always exist, whether or not it is desirable that they should, what place they occupy in this world, what their place should be...."

But first we must ask: what is a woman? "Tota mulier in utero," says one, "woman is a womb." But in speaking of certain women, **connoisseurs** declare that they are not women, although they are equipped with a uterus like the rest. All agree in recognizing the fact that females exist in the human species; today as always they make up about one half of humanity. And yet we are told that femininity is in danger; we are exhorted to be women, remain women, become women. It would appear, then, that every female human being is not necessarily a woman; to be so considered she must share in that mysterious and threatened reality known as femininity. Is this attribute something secreted by the **ovaries**? Or is it a **Platonic** essence, a product of the philosophic imagination? Is a rustling petticoat enough to bring it down to earth? Although some women try zealously to **incarnate** this essence, it is hardly patentable. It is frequently described in vague and dazzling terms that seem to have been borrowed from the vocabulary of the **seers**....

The biological and social sciences no longer admit the existence of unchangeably fixed entities that determine given characteristics, such as those ascribed to woman, the Jew, or the Negro. Science regards any characteristic as a reaction dependent in part upon a situation. If today femininity no longer exists, then it never existed. But does the word woman, then, have no specific content?... Many American women particularly

Erudite: Learned.

Connoisseurs: Persons with informed judgments on specific topics.

Ovaries: The part of the female reproductive system that produces eggs.

Platonic: Beyond purely sexual passion; named for the ideas of ancient Greek philosopher Plato.

Incarnate: To give bodily human form and characteristics.

Seers: Prophets.

are prepared to think that there is no longer any place for woman as such; if a backward individual still takes herself for a woman, her friends advise her to be psychoanalyzed and thus get rid of this obsession.... Surely woman is, like man, a human being; but such a declaration is abstract. The fact is that every concrete human being is always a singular, separate individual. To decline to accept such notions as the eternal feminine, the black soul, the Jewish character, is not to deny that Jews, Negroes, women exist today—this denial does not represent a liberation for those concerned, but rather a flight from reality. Some years ago a well-known woman writer refused to permit her portrait to appear in a series of photographs especially devoted to women writers; she wished to be counted among the men. But in order to gain this privilege she made use of her husband's influence! Women who assert that they are men lay claim none the less to masculine consideration and respect. I recall also a young **Trotskyite** standing on a platform at a boisterous meeting and getting ready to use her fists, in spite of her evident fragility. She was denying her feminine weakness; but it was for love of a militant male whose equal she wished to be. The attitude of defiance of many American women proves that they are haunted by a sense of their femininity. In truth, to go for a walk with one's eyes open is enough to demonstrate that humanity is divided into two classes of individuals whose clothes, faces, bodies, smiles, gaits, interests, and occupations are manifestly different. Perhaps these differences are superficial, perhaps they are destined to disappear. What is certain is that right now they do most obviously exist.

If her functioning as a female is not enough to define woman, if we decline also to explain her through "the eternal feminine," and if nevertheless we admit, provisionally, that women do exist, then we must face the question: what is a woman?

To state the question is, to me, to suggest, at once, a preliminary answer. The fact that I ask it is in itself significant. A man would never get the notion of writing a book on the peculiar sit-

Trotskyite: *Follower of the Russian Jewish revolutionary Leon Trotsky.*

de Beauvoir

Simone de Beauvoir

Simone de Beauvoir (1908-1986) was born in Paris, France, the oldest of two girls in a middle-class family. As the daughter of a devoutly Roman Catholic mother and an agnostic (a person who doesn't believe humans can know whether God exists) father, she experienced a clash of consciousness over the issue of religion and decided early in her teens that she no longer believed in the existence of God. A student of literature and philosophy, de Beauvoir received her degree from the Sorbonne, University of Paris, in 1929. She taught at various colleges until 1943, when she devoted herself to writing full time. De Beauvoir and her longtime partner, philosopher Jean-Paul Sartre, were influential in the existentialist movement, a school of thought that centers on the isolation of the individual's experience in an indifferent and purposeless world. During her life de Beauvoir published more than 20 books, among them works of fiction, autobiographical writings, and philosophical essays.

uation of the human male. But if I wish to define myself, I must first of all say: "I am a woman"; on this truth must be based all further discussion. A man never begins by presenting himself as an individual of a certain sex; it goes without saying that he is a man. The terms masculine and feminine are used symmetrically only as a matter of form, as on legal papers. In actuality the relation of the two sexes is not quite like that of two electrical poles, for man represents both the positive and the neutral, as is indicated by the common use of man to designate human beings in general; whereas woman represents only the negative, defined by limiting criteria.… In the midst of an abstract discussion it is **vexing** to hear a man say: "You think thus and so because you are a woman"; but I know that my only defense is to reply: "I think thus and so because it is true," thereby removing my subjective self from the argument. It would be out of the question to reply: "And you think the contrary because you are a man," for it is understood that the fact of being a man is no peculiarity. A man is in the right in being a man; it is the woman who is in the wrong.… There is an absolute human type, the masculine. Woman has ovaries, a uterus; these peculiarities imprison her in her subjectivity, **circumscribe** her within the limits of her own nature. It is often said that she thinks with her glands. Man superbly ignores the fact that his anatomy also includes glands, such as the testicles, and that they secrete hormones. He thinks of his body as a direct and normal connection with the world, which he believes he apprehends objectively, whereas he regards the body of woman as a hindrance, a prison, weighed down by everything peculiar to it. "The female is a female by virtue of a certain lack of qualities," said [ancient Greek philosopher] Aristotle; "we should regard the female nature as afflicted with a natural defectiveness." And St. Thomas for his part pronounced woman to be an "imperfect man," an "incidental" being. This is symbolized in **Genesis** where Eve is depicted as made from what Bossuet called "a **supernumerary** bone" of Adam.

Thus humanity is male and man defines woman not in herself but as relative to him; she is not regarded as an **autonomous** being.… And she is simply what man decrees; thus she is called "the sex," by which is meant that she appears essentially to the male as a sexual being. For him she is sex—absolute sex, no less. She is defined and differentiated with reference to man and not he with reference to her; she is the incidental, the inessential as opposed to the essential. He is the Subject, he is the Absolute—she is the Other.…

Vexing: Causing distress, trouble, or annoyance.

Circumscribe: To define or constrict with boundaries.

Genesis: The first book of the Old Testament of the Bible; it tells the story of creation.

Supernumerary: Extra.

Autonomous: Existing independently; having self-direction, freedom, and moral independence.

de Beauvoir

It is nonsense to assert that **revelry**, vice, ecstasy, passion, would become impossible if man and woman were equal in concrete matters; ... in sexuality will always be materialized the tension, the anguish, the joy, the frustration, and the triumph of existence. To **emancipate** woman is to refuse to confine her to the relations she bears to man, not to deny them to her; let her have her independent existence and she will continue none the less to exist for him also: mutually recognizing each other as subject, each will yet remain for the other an other. The **reciprocity** of their relations will not do away with the miracles—desire, possession, love, dream, adventure—worked by the division of human beings into two separate categories; and the words that move us—giving, conquering, uniting—will not lose their meaning. On the contrary, when we abolish the slavery of half of humanity, together with the whole system of hypocrisy that it implies, then the "division" of humanity will reveal its genuine significance and the human couple will find its true form. "The direct, natural, necessary relation of human creatures is the relation of man to woman," [German political philosopher Karl] Marx has said [in his Philosophical Works, Vol. VI]. "The nature of this relation determines to what point man himself is to be considered as a generic being, as mankind; the relation of man to woman is the most natural relation of human being to human being. By it is shown, therefore, to what point the natural behavior of man has become human or to what point the human being has become his natural being, to what point his human nature has become his nature."

The case could not be better stated. It is for man to establish the reign of liberty in the midst of the world of the given. To gain the supreme victory, it is necessary, for one thing, that by and through their natural differentiation men and women **unequivocally affirm** their brotherhood. (de Beauvoir, pp. xv-xix, 813-14)

Revelry: *Partying.*
Emancipate: *Free.*
Reciprocity: *Mutual dependence or exchange.*
Unequivocally affirm: *State positively and without doubt.*

What happened next...

The controversial book *The Second Sex* helped inspire the emerging women's rights movement in the United States and France during the 1960s and 1970s. After its publication de Beauvoir became increasingly involved in the "Mouvement de liberation des femmes." In 1971 she and other prominent women signed a manifesto acknowledging that they had had illegal abortions. This *Manifeste des 343* generated publicity as part of a campaign to change the laws forbidding abortions. Around the same time de Beauvoir served as president of the League for the Rights of Women, which lobbied for legislation to aid battered wives, working women, and single parents. Today *The Second Sex* remains a classic analysis of womanhood in Western society.

Did you know...

- Simone de Beauvoir first met philosopher Jean-Paul Sartre when they studied together for oral exams at the Sorbonne in 1929. Sartre took first place with the highest national scores; de Beauvoir took second place.

- Although they never married—neither one felt compelled to limit themselves by engaging in the institution of marriage or the process of childrearing—de Beauvoir and Sartre were companions for 51 years. Sartre affectionately called his lifetime lover by the nickname "Castor," the French word for "beaver." Back in their school days, one of their friends commented that "beauvoir" sounded like the English word "beaver," and the nickname stuck.

- De Beauvoir's novel *The Mandarins,* about intellectuals living in France after World War II, won the prestigious Prix Goncourt in 1954.

For Further Reading

De Beauvoir, Simone. *The Second Sex.* Translated and edited by H. M. Parshley. New York: Knopf, 1953. Reprinted. New York: Random House, 1974.

Keefe, Terry. *Simone de Beauvoir: A Study of Her Writings.* London: Harrap Ltd., 1983.

Rossi, Alice S., ed. *The Feminist Papers: From Adams to de Beauvoir.* New York: Columbia University Press, 1973.

The Feminine Mystique

From the text written by Betty Friedan
Published in 1963

U.S. feminist leader and author Betty Friedan is a founding member of the American women's liberation movement of the 1960s and 1970s. Her book *The Feminine Mystique* helped launch a resurgence of interest in women's rights. Published in 1963, *The Feminine Mystique* examines society's role in the perpetuation of a myth—the myth that women should achieve complete fulfillment in their domestic roles as homemaker, wife, and mother. Expecting only modest success, her publisher printed only two thousand copies of the first edition; within ten years, however, three million copies of the hardcover edition had been sold. Friedan's book seemed to capture a sense of the profound discontent felt by many women. The outpouring of response surprised everyone in America, including the author herself.

Friedan based *The Feminine Mystique* largely on her own experiences. She lived in a comfortable suburban home, took care of her husband and three children, and wrote articles for women's magazines such as the *Ladies' Home Journal.* She was

Friedan at a 1978 march
to extend the deadline
for ERA ratification.

dissatisfied with her life but felt that society expected her to be completely fulfilled. Unsure if other women experienced similar discontent, she sent a survey in 1957 to her fellow classmates from Smith College. The results convinced Friedan that many women were also suffering quietly. Using her college background in psychology and her experience as a newspaper reporter, Friedan began extensive research on "the problem that has no name."

To understand what was happening in American society, Friedan looked to the past. She studied the content of articles, advertisements, and advice columns from journals and newspapers of past decades to see what messages women were receiving. In a similarly systematic way, she critiqued television programs and advertisements. Interviews with experts in advertising, psychology, sociology, and education helped her to piece together a disturbing picture: all forms of media, from television to print, gave American women the same message—that her most honorable and, in fact, *only* role was that of being a happy housewife and mother. Friedan called this powerful and pervasive image the "feminine mystique." Since society expected women to conform to this ideal image, many were ashamed to admit their deep dissatisfaction with their lot in life.

At first Friedan tried to publish her thoughts as a magazine article. However, the very same women's magazines she routinely wrote for in the past rejected her ideas. For five years Friedan juggled the demands of her family while she researched and wrote. In 1963 she completed *The Feminine Mystique,* the book that would help ignite the "women's lib" movement in America.

Things to Remember While Reading
The Feminine Mystique:

- Friedan observes profound changes in American society after World War II, with women—even those with college educations—concentrating solely on their responsibilities as homemakers, wives, and mothers.

- According to Friedan, the "feminine mystique" encourages women to forsake an independent identity. Television and magazine advertising perpetuate unrealistic stereotypes of femininity by portraying an ideal image women should try to achieve.

- The author notes that her peers and the women of the generation before them sacrificed their goals by placing the needs of their families above everything. Significant changes throughout society must occur in order for women to move beyond the confining domestic sphere..

The Feminine Mystique

The problem lay buried, unspoken, for many years in the minds of American women. It was a strange stirring, a sense of dissatisfaction, a yearning that women suffered in the middle of the twentieth century in the United States. Each suburban wife struggled with it alone. As she made the beds, shopped for groceries, matched slipcover material, ate peanut butter sandwiches with her children, chauffeured Cub Scouts and Brownies, lay beside her husband at night—she was afraid to ask even of herself the silent question—"Is this all?"

For over fifteen years there was no word of this yearning in the millions of words written about women, for women, in all the columns, books and articles by experts telling women their role was to seek fulfillment as wives and mothers. Over and over women heard in voices of tradition and of Freudian [relating to the theories of the Austrian psychoanalyst Sigmund Freud, who pioneered a method of uninhibited self-expression known as "free association." This type of "talking cure" allows patients to express their unconscious desires and thereby work through their emotional problems] sophistication that they could desire no greater destiny than to glory in their own femininity. Experts told them how to catch a man and keep him, how to breastfeed children and handle their toilet training, how to cope with sibling rivalry and adolescent rebellion; how to buy a dishwasher, bake bread, cook gourmet snails, and build a swimming pool with their own hands; how to dress, look, and act more feminine and make marriage more exciting; how to keep their husbands from dying young and their sons from growing into delinquents. They were taught to pity the neurotic, unfeminine, unhappy women who wanted to be poets or physicists or presidents. They learned that truly feminine women do not want careers, higher education, political rights—the independence and the opportunities that the old-fashioned feminists fought for. Some women, in their forties and fifties, still remembered painfully giving up those dreams, but most of the younger women no longer even thought about them. A thousand expert voices applauded their femininity, their adjustment, their new maturity. All they had to do was devote their lives from earliest girlhood to finding a husband and bearing children.

By the end of the nineteen-fifties, the average marriage age of women in America dropped to 20, and was still dropping, into the teens. Fourteen million girls were engaged by 17. The proportion of women attending college in comparison with men [dropped] from 47 per cent in 1920 to 35 per cent in 1958. A century earlier, women had fought for higher education; now girls went to college to get a husband. By the mid-fifties, 60 per cent dropped out of college to marry.... Colleges built dormitories for "married students," but the students were almost always the husbands. A new degree was instituted for the wives—"Ph.T." (Putting Husband Through).

*Then American girls began getting married in high school. And the women's magazines, **deploring** the unhappy statistics about these young marriages, urged that courses on marriage, and marriage counselors, be installed in the high schools. Girls started going steady at twelve and thirteen, in junior high. Manufacturers put out brassieres with false bosoms of foam rubber for little girls of ten. And an advertisement for a child's dress, sizes 3-6x, in the New York Times in the fall of 1960, said: "She Too Can Join the Man-Trap Set."*

*By the end of the fifties, the United States birthrate was overtaking India's.... Statisticians were especially astounded at the fantastic increase in the number of babies among college women. Where once they had two children, now they had four, five, six. Women who had once wanted careers were now making careers out of having babies. So rejoiced Life magazine in a 1956 **paean** to the movement of American women back to the home.*

*In a New York hospital, a woman had a nervous breakdown when she found she could not breastfeed her baby. In other hospitals, women dying of cancer refused a drug which research proved might save their lives: its side effects were said to be unfeminine. "If I have only one life, let me live it as a blonde," a larger-than-life-sized picture of a pretty, **vacuous** woman proclaimed from newspaper, magazine, and drugstore ads. And across America, three out of every ten women*

Deploring: Expressing grief or regret.

Paean: A tribute or hymn of praise.

Vacuous: Empty; lacking intelligence; stupid.

National Organization for Women

The National Organization for Women (NOW) was founded in 1966 to help promote full equality for both women and men. The group formed in direct response to the failure of the Equal Employment Opportunity Commission (EEOC) to prosecute cases of discrimination against women. When the EEOC failed to respond to complaints filed by women, a group of female leaders decided to create a female-centered lobby group similar to the National Association for the Advancement of Colored People (NAACP). The original 28 women who formed NOW included Betty Friedan, author of *The Feminine Mystique*.

NOW played an instrumental role in the congressional passage of the Equal Rights Amendment (ERA) in 1972. However, after ten years of hard work, the ERA fell short of the 38 states required for ratification in 1982. Still, by the dawn of the twenty-first century NOW had achieved many of its goals, including winning the right to paid maternity leave, deductions for child care expenses, legalized abortion, and EEOC enforcement of the Civil Rights Act.

dyed their hair blonde. They ate a chalk called Metrecal, instead of food, to shrink to the size of the thin young models. Department-store buyers reported that American women, since 1939, had become three and four sizes smaller. "Women are out to fit the clothes, instead of vice-versa," one buyer said.

Interior decorators were designing kitchens with mosaic murals and original paintings, for kitchens were once again the center of women's lives. Home sewing became a million-dollar industry. Many women no longer left their homes, except to shop, chauffeur their children, or attend a social engagement with their husbands. Girls were growing up in America without ever having jobs outside the home. In the late fifties, a sociological phenomenon was suddenly remarked: a third of American women now worked, but most were no longer young and very few were pursuing careers. They were married women who held part-time jobs, selling or secretarial, to put

their husbands through school, their sons through college, or to help pay the mortgage. Or they were widows supporting families. Fewer and fewer women were entering professional work. The shortages in the nursing, social work, and teaching professions caused crises in almost every American city. Concerned over the Soviet Union's lead in the space race, scientists noted that America's greatest source of unused brain-power was women. But girls would not study physics: it was "unfeminine." A girl refused a science fellowship at Johns Hopkins to take a job in a real-estate office. All she wanted, she said, was what every other American girl wanted—to get married, have four children and live in a nice house in a nice suburb.

The suburban housewife—she was the dream image of the young American women and the envy, it was said, of women all over the world. The American housewife—freed by science and labor-saving appliances from the drudgery, the

NOW members protesting the treatment of women outside the Saudi Embassy in 1990.

dangers of childbirth and the illnesses of her grandmother. She was healthy, beautiful, educated, concerned only about her husband, her children, her home. She had found true feminine fulfillment. As a housewife and mother, she was respected as a full and equal partner to man in his world. She was free to choose automobiles, clothes, appliances, supermarkets; she had everything that women ever dreamed of....

The feminine mystique permits, even encourages, women to ignore the question of their identity. The mystique says they can answer the question "Who am I?" by saying "Tom's wife ... Mary's mother." But I don't think the mystique would have such power over American women if they did not fear to face this terrifying blank which makes them unable to see themselves after twenty-one. The truth is—and how long it has been true, I'm not sure, but it was true in my generation and it is true of girls growing up today [in the early 1960s]—an American woman no longer has a private image to tell her who she is, or can be, or wants to be.

The public image, in the magazines and television commercials, is designed to sell washing machines, cake mixes, deodorants, detergents, rejuvenating face creams, hair tints. But the power of that image, on which companies spend millions of dollars for television time and ad space, comes from this: American women no longer know who they are. They are sorely in need of a new image to help them find their identity. As the motivational researchers keep telling the advertisers, American women are so unsure of who they should be that they look to this glossy public image to decide every detail of their lives. They look for the image they will no longer take from their mothers.

In my generation, many of us knew that we did not want to be like our mothers, even when we loved them. We could not help but see their disappointment. Did we understand, or only resent, the sadness, the emptiness, that made them hold too fast to us, try to live our lives, run our fathers' lives, spend their days shopping or yearning for things that never seemed to satisfy them, no matter how much money they cost? Strangely, many mothers who loved their daughters—and mine was one—did not want their daughters to grow up like them either. They knew we needed something more.

But even if they urged, insisted, fought to help us educate ourselves, even if they talked with yearnings of careers that were not open to them, they could not give us an image of what we could be. They could only tell us that their lives were too empty, tied to home; that children, cooking, clothes, bridge, and charities were not enough. A mother might tell her daughter, spell it out, "Don't be just a housewife like me." But that daughter, sensing that her mother was too frustrated to savor the love of her husband and children, might feel: "I will succeed where my mother failed, I will fulfill myself as a woman," and never read the lesson of her mother's life. (Friedan, The Feminine Mystique, pp. 11-13, 64-65)

What happened next...

Betty Friedan was one of 28 women who founded the National Organization for Women (NOW) in 1966. The women decided to form a political lobbying group in response to the U.S. government's failure to enforce Title VII of the Civil Rights Act of 1964, which prohibits sexual discrimination in employment. At the first NOW organizing meeting, members elected Friedan as president. They also drafted the NOW charter, demanding "fully equal partnership of the sexes, as part of the worldwide revolution of human rights." Growing to 15,000 members during its first five years, NOW became the leading voice in the women's liberation movement. In addition, Friedan helped form the National Woman's Political Caucus in 1971, an organization that seeks to increase the number of women participating in the political process as candidates and voters.

Betty Friedan

Betty Friedan (1921—) was born Betty Goldstein, the oldest of three children, in Peoria, Illinois. She excelled in high school, started the school's literary magazine, and was valedictorian of her class. In 1942 she graduated summa cum laude from Smith College with a degree in psychology. Friedan continued her studies in psychology with the help of two research fellowships to the University of California at Berkeley. After deciding not to pursue her doctorate, she moved to New York City, worked as a journalist, and in 1947 married Carl Friedan. Before divorcing in 1969, the couple had three children. Aside from *The Feminine Mystique* (1963), Friedan also wrote *It Changed My Life* (1976), *The Second Stage* (1981), and *The Fountain of Age* (1993).

Did you know...

- In the late 1960s Friedan took legal action against airlines for their deplorable employment policies, which—among other things—forced stewardesses to resign at age 30 or when they married.

- Friedan led a large nationwide protest, "Women's Strike for Equality," on August 26, 1970, the fiftieth anniversary of women winning the right to vote. The strike focused attention on the continuing struggle for women's equality in areas such as equal employment and educational opportunities.

- Her 1993 book *The Fountain of Age* examines "the mystique of aging" and the negative image society has of older men and women. This work reviews age discrimination much as *The Feminist Mystique* discusses the obstacles facing women.

For Further Reading

Friedan, Betty. *The Feminine Mystique.* New York: Dell Publishing, 1963, reprinted, 1974.

Friedan, Betty. *It Changed My Life.* New York: Random House, 1976.

Sisterhood, 1972

Night Thoughts of a Media Watcher, 1980-81

Selections from Outrageous Acts and Everyday Rebellions
Written by Gloria Steinem
Originally collected and published in 1983

During the women's liberation movement of the 1960s and 1970s, feminist-journalist Gloria Steinem became a popular symbol of American women's demand for change. She attracted considerable national attention with her articulate and passionate defense of women's rights. The media apparently followed Steinem's every move closely, for she was an attractive, single woman—and therefore an easy target for scrutiny and criticism.

Thousands of women joined the movement Betty Friedan ignited with her 1963 book *The Feminine Mystique.* But Steinem did not want this powerful social "revolution" to be labeled merely as a "white-middle-class movement." Determined to widen its public image, she traveled extensively for several years with black feminists to give public lectures across the country. Her co-lecturers included child-care pioneer Dorothy Pitman Hughes, feminist lawyer Florynce Kennedy, and writer Margaret Sloan. Steinem's goal of increasing awareness about the discrimination facing all women—regardless of race, econom-

ic status, or sexual orientation—caused controversy within and outside the women's movement.

In 1971 Steinem helped created the first female-controlled national magazine for women readers. She invited a group of feminist journalists and writers to her home in New York City to discuss how they could reach more American women. They decided to develop a different type of publication, one that would redefine the typical content of women's magazines. Instead of recipes and beauty columns, the new magazine—called *Ms.*—would cover feminist issues and ideas. Steinem and her fellow journalists aimed to share the ideas of the women's movement with all women, even those who did not consider themselves feminists. Despite their lack of funding, the group also decided to reject all advertising that portrayed women offensively.

Steinem arranged for a preview copy of *Ms.* to be distributed as an insert in *New York* magazine in December 1971. She and her co-founders planned to sell the preview copy on the

Steinem and former Congresswoman Bella Abzug show their support for a 1979 anti-inflation campaign.

newsstands for three months as they scrambled to produce the next issue. All 300,000 copies sold out in eight days. More than 20,000 letters poured in from women across the country praising the arrival of the first magazine controlled editorially and financially by women.

In 1983 Steinem published a collection of her articles from *Ms.* magazine in her book *Outrageous Acts and Everyday Rebellions.* The article "Sisterhood," excerpted below, was first published in 1972 and the essay "Night Thoughts of a Media Watcher" appeared in the November 1981 issue.

Things to Remember While Reading Steinem's Essays from *Outrageous Acts and Everyday Rebellions*:

- As an early spokesperson for women's rights, Steinem encountered much resistance but found support and encouragement from other women, whom she refers to as her "sisters."

- Efforts had been under way since the 1920s to pass an Equal Rights Amendment (ERA), a federal constitutional amendment for women's rights. Five decades later the amendment—which read, "Equality of rights under the law shall not be denied or abridged by the United States or by any State on account of sex"—passed both houses of Congress but failed to gain support of the 38 states necessary for ratification.

- Steinem gives her account of the media's coverage of the ERA struggle that took place during the 1970s and early 1980s. Although most Americans supported the ERA, the media were accused of giving too much attention to its few opponents.

- "Night Thoughts of a Media Watcher" shows the author's insightfulness as a social observer. She claims that women, like gamblers, take a chance whenever they marry. Many women at the time (the 1970s and early 1980s) depended solely on their husbands for economic support; but men's success, though critically important, was never guaranteed. Until women achieve full equality, she argues, their husbands will always determine their fate.

Sisterhood

At first my discoveries seemed personal. In fact, they were the same ones so many millions of women have made and are continuing to make. Greatly simplified, they go like this: Women are human beings first, with minor differences from men that apply largely to the single act of reproduction. We share the dreams, capabilities, and weaknesses of all human beings, but our occasional pregnancies and other visible differences have been used—even more pervasively, if less brutally, than racial differences have been used—to create an "inferior" group and an elaborate division of labor. This division is continued for a clear if often unconscious reason: the economic and social profit of **patriarchy** males as a group.

Once this feminist realization dawned, I reacted in what turned out to be predictable ways. First, I was amazed at the simplicity and obviousness of a revelation that made sense, at last, of my life experience.... Second, I realized how far this new vision of life was from the system around us, and how tough it would be to explain a feminist realization at all, much less to get people (especially, though not only, men) to contemplate so drastic a change.

But I tried to explain. God knows (she knows) that women try....

We even use logic. If a woman spends a year bearing and nursing a child, for instance, she is supposed to have the primary responsibility for raising that child to adulthood. That's logic by the male definition, but it often forces women to accept raising children as their only function, keeps them from doing any other kind of work, or discourages them from being mothers at all. Wouldn't it be just as logical to say that a child has two parents, therefore both are equally responsible for child rearing—and the father should compensate for that

Patriarchy: *A system of social organization dominated by men.*

extra year by spending more than half the time caring for the child? Logic is in the eye of the logician.

Occasionally, these efforts at explaining actually succeed. More often, I get the feeling that most women are speaking **Urdu** and most men are speaking **Pali**.

Whether joyful or painful, both kinds of reaction to our discovery have a great reward. They give birth to sisterhood.

First, we share the exhilaration of growth and self-discovery.... Whether we are giving other women this new knowledge or receiving it from them, the pleasure for all concerned is very moving.

In the second stage, when we're exhausted from dredging up facts and arguments for the men whom we had previously thought advanced and intelligent, we make another simple discovery: many women understand. We may share experiences, make jokes, paint pictures, and describe humiliations that mean little to men, but women understand.

The odd thing about these deep and personal connections among women living under patriarchy is that they often leap barriers of age, economics, worldly experience, race, culture —all the barriers that, in male or mixed society, seem so impossible to cross....

The status quo protects itself by punishing all challengers, especially women whose rebellion strikes at the most fundamental social organization: the sex roles that convince half the population that its identity depends on being first in work or in war, and the other half that it must serve worldwide as unpaid or underpaid labor....

Any woman who chooses to behave like a full human being should be warned that the armies of the status quo will treat her as something of a dirty joke. Ridicule is their natural and first weapon, with more serious opposition to follow. She will need sisterhood.

All of that is meant to be a warning, but not a discouragement. There are more rewards than punishments....

—1972 (Steinem, pp. 122-27)

Urdu: An Indic language; the official literary language of Pakistan; used by Moslems in India.

Pali: An ancient Indic language used in Hinayana Buddhism.

Steinem

Night Thoughts of a Media Watcher

Steinem and Betty Friedan sign a telegram asking President Carter to support the ERA.

The Equal Rights Amendment [ERA] began its long ratification process in 1972, yet to my knowledge, not one major newspaper or radio station, not one network news department or national television show, has ever done an independent investigative report on what the ERA will and will not do.

Instead, the major media have been content to present occasional ... contradictory reports from those who are for or against. One expert is quoted as saying that the ERA will strengthen the legal rights of women in general and homemakers in particular by causing the courts to view marriage as a partnership, and the next one says the ERA will force wives to work outside the home and eliminate support payments. One political leader explains on camera that the ERA

*protects women and men from discriminatory federal laws;
then another politician calls the ERA a federal power grab
that will reduce individual rights. One activist says that the
ERA is a simple guarantee of democracy that should have
been part of the Bill of Rights, ... and the next one insists it
will destroy the family, eliminate heterosexuality, and integrate
bathrooms.*

*Understandably, the audience is confused.... It's true that
the majority of women and men have continued to support
the ERA (by a margin that has increased since the [Ronald] Rea-
gan administration demonstrated that progress could be
reversed without it), but I'm not sure the media can take much
credit for that fact. There is some evidence that 50-50, so-
called objective reporting has actually* impeded *the building of
a larger majority.*

*For instance, reading or hearing the actual twenty-four
words of the ERA is the most reliable path to its support. Many
people are still surprised to learn that there's no mention of uni-
sex or abortion or combat* in its text; *such is the confusion
created by anti-ERA arguments. Yet most ERA news coverage
never quotes its text at all.*

*Among reporters and news executives, however, there is
great self-righteousness. They have followed the so-called fair-
ness doctrine. They have presented "both sides of the issue" by
devoting the same number of minutes or amount of space to the
"pro" and the "con." This has remained true, even though
majority support for the ERA means a "con" is often tough to
find. I've frequently been called by an interviewer and asked,
"Would you bring an 'anti' with you?"*

*One result of this prizefight school of journalism is that
Phyllis Schlafly, who was not a nationally famous person pre-
ERA, has become the only name that most Americans can
think of when asked what women oppose it.... Another result
is the idea that women* voted *against the ERA; not the two
dozen or so aging white male state legislators, plus econom-*

Phyllis Schlafly and the ERA

Phyllis Schlafly was probably the most vocal opponent of the Equal Rights Amendment (ERA). According to Schlafly, the ERA would erode the family unit and ultimately eradicate, or remove, certain special privileges enjoyed by women. She made homemakers the primary targets of her anti-ERA message, convincing them that passage of the amendment would result in devastating changes. In the *Phyllis Schlafly Report,* Schlafly wrote that under the terms of the ERA American woman would give up fundamental privileges, including the right "(1) to NOT take a job, (2) to keep her baby, and (3) to be supported by her husband." Based at her home in Illinois, Schlafly helped create a powerful lobby group with thousands of members. She campaigned against the ERA by traveling throughout the country and publishing the *Eagle Forum Newsletter* and the *Phyllis Schlafly Report.*

ic and religious interests, who are the actual culprits. A third result is the notion that black Americans don't support the ERA, though black state legislators have voted overwhelmingly for it. If black women and men had been represented in legislatures in proportion to their present numbers in the population, especially in southern states, the ERA would have passed long ago....

Gloria Steinem

Gloria Steinem (1934—) was born in Toledo, Ohio, the youngest of two girls. She graduated magna cum laude from Smith College in 1956 with a major in government. For two years after her graduation from college, Steinem studied in India at the universities of Delhi and Calcutta. In 1958, she moved to New York City and became a freelance writer for women's magazines and television. Ten years later she began writing a political column for *New York* magazine.

In 1971 Steinem helped organize the National Woman's Political Caucus, an organization that encourages political activity by women. Shortly thereafter she founded *Ms.* magazine and served as its editor for 15 years. Besides *Outrageous Acts and Everyday Rebellions* (1983), Steinem also wrote *The Beach Book* (1963), *The Revolution Within* (1992), and *Moving Beyond Words* (1994).

It isn't that ... independent reporting [on the facts about the ERA] would be difficult. More than fifty years of legislative history is available to explain the impact intended by Congress. An issue of the Yale Law Journal *and many authoritative books have been devoted to projecting its impact in scholarly detail.... Pennsylvania adopted its ERA more than a decade ago, and bathrooms have not been integrated, abortion and homosexual rights have not been affected, for better or worse. On the other hand, women's economic rights have been strengthened; equality in education, employment, and insurance benefits has advanced; and sex-based discriminatory laws against men also have been struck down.*

So why haven't independent, in-depth reports been done?... Why do [the media] allow legislators to vote against the majority opinion ... without fearing a journalistic expose...?

Ask them. A future with or without the ERA is at stake. And so is good or lousy journalism....

I've noticed that, from the novels of Dostoevsky [Russian author Fyodor Dostoevsky, known for his realistic, radical writings, especially Crime and Punishment] *to the television shows about Las Vegas, big-time gambling is portrayed as a male-only obsession. Someone once asked me why women don't gamble as much as men do. I gave the commonsensical reply that we don't have as much money. That was a true but incomplete answer. In fact, women's total instinct for gambling has been satisfied by marriage.*

If men doubt the magnitude of the gamble, consider just how tough it is to know that someone you are about to marry, who may be, by tradition and by lack of economic alternative, your lifetime identity and meal ticket, is going to have the law career or foreman's job or political office that you want for yourself and for your security. Not so easy, right?

In the fifties, I remember college friends taking their fiancé's poems, architectural drawings, or senior thesis to the appropriate professor and asking, "Is this guy any good?"

Of course, this gamble has been diminished by our increased ability to support ourselves. But until pay and power are equal, and women no longer have to take on men's names and career identities, it's not going to end.

—1980, 1981

(Steinem, pp. 356-59)

What happened next...

By 1982 subscriptions to *Ms.* numbered 200,000. After serving as the magazine's editor for 15 years, Steinem resigned in 1987 to pursue other activities, including several book projects. But during the politically conservative era of the 1980s, economic difficulties began to threaten the magazine's existence. In 1988 *Ms.* ownership changed to a more financially secure publisher. Under the guidance of a new owner, the publication became slightly more mainstream but continued to feature women writers and cover issues important to women's equality. *Ms.* later changed hands again, becoming an ad-free, bimonthly magazine supported by its subscribers. Besides serving as a consulting editor for the magazine, Steinem continues to give lectures, appear at book-signings, and campaign for political candidates.

Did you know...

- During her senior year at Smith College, Steinem received a fellowship for postgraduate study in India. To help support herself while overseas, she wrote *The Thousand Indias* for the government tourist bureau in 1957.

- Steinem accepted an undercover reporting assignment to work as a Playboy bunny in 1963. In a two-part article published in *Show* magazine, she described the demeaning labor practices she had witnessed. Her article caused considerable controversy, and she became the target of vicious attacks in the media.

- In 1986 Steinem wrote a book about the tragic life and death of bombshell Marilyn Monroe called *Marilyn: Norma Jean.*

For Further Reading

Heilbrun, Carolyn G. *The Education of a Woman: The Life of Gloria Steinem.* New York: Dial Press, 1995.

Steinem, Gloria. *Outrageous Acts and Everyday Rebellions.* New York: Henry Holt, 1983. Reprinted with new preface and notes by the author, 1995.

Reproductive Rights

A woman's reproductive rights—to practice birth control and obtain an abortion if she chooses—continued to spark controversy at the close of the twentieth century. But up until the late 1800s state and federal laws did not generally interfere with such matters. Everything changed in 1873, when antivice crusader Anthony Comstock helped persuade Congress to pass a law prohibiting the distribution of information concerning contraception and abortion. The **Comstock Law**, as his proposal came to be called, was the basis by which the U.S. government restricted information it regarded as indecent.

Between 1900 and 1920 women began to demand more control over their lives by practicing contraception (the prevention of pregnancies). Activist **Emma Goldman** included discussions on family planning in her speeches and became one of the first women to challenge the validity of the Comstock Law. Attorney and feminist **Crystal Eastman** argued that the right to plan and prevent pregnancy was an essential element of a woman's right to self-determination. Eastman also had the foresight to realize that women's growing access to employment opportunities would lead to difficult choices in balancing professional and family responsibilities. She believed that family planning was an integral part of any woman's plan to achieve economic security.

New York City nurse **Margaret Sanger** saw firsthand the economic hardship that women and their families faced when they did not practice some form of birth control. While working among poor immigrant families, she witnessed poverty-induced hunger, the physical strain of repeated childbearing, and the deadly effects of illegal and unsafe abortion attempts. Sanger, who coined the phrase "birth control," distributed information in her magazine titled the *Woman Rebel.* She also published the *Birth Control Review* and founded the American Birth Control League, which later became Planned Parenthood.

Legal institutions were slow to recognize a woman's right to privacy—and therefore to practice birth control. The Supreme Court finally recognized a married couple's right to use contraceptives in the 1965 case of *Griswold vs. Connecticut.* In the landmark 1973 **Roe vs. Wade** decision, the Supreme Court ruled that a woman's constitutional right to privacy gives her the freedom to choose whether or not to have an abortion in the first trimester of pregnancy. Since 1973 the Supreme Court has sought to clarify various aspects of abortion rights, including the need for a mandatory waiting period prior to obtaining an abortion and the use of public funds to pay for the procedure.

While feminists argue for a woman's right to self-determination, pro-life advocates champion the rights of the unborn. Pro-life organizations such as **Operation Rescue** practice civil disobedience and support political candidates to advance their position. The Catholic Church has also contributed to the debate concerning reproductive rights with its 1968 papal encyclical *Humanae Vitae.* In this official decree Pope Paul VI prohibited Roman Catholics from utilizing any form of birth control other than natural timing (refraining from intercourse during a woman's fertile time).

The heated controversy over family planning ties in with scientists' predictions about Earth's expanding population—

and the threat it poses to the existence of the human species. In his book *The Population Bomb*, **Paul R. Ehrlich** asserts that the planet simply cannot sustain continued population growth. These projections add another dimension—the environmental perspective—to the ongoing debate concerning reproductive rights.

Victims of Morality

Speech delivered by Emma Goldman
c. 1913

Controversial feminist and political activist Emma Goldman was an early champion of birth control. Her lifelong commitment to anarchism—a rejection of the authority of a centralized government in favor of a cooperative society—led her to support many radical causes that challenged accepted American beliefs and morals. Anarchism grew in response to the industrial forces shaping society during the late nineteenth century and early twentieth century. Goldman and her compatriots feared that the increase in large factories, the growth of big corporations, and a tightening of the reins of government suppressed their individual rights and exploited them as workers. Anarchism differed from communism and socialism by advocating the end of *all* forms of government and institutions. (Communism is a system of government in which the state controls the means of production and the distribution of goods; socialism is a political doctrine that champions the removal of private property in a quest to attain a classless society.) Instead of reforming society, Goldman and other anarchists sought to recreate it—to form an ideal society.

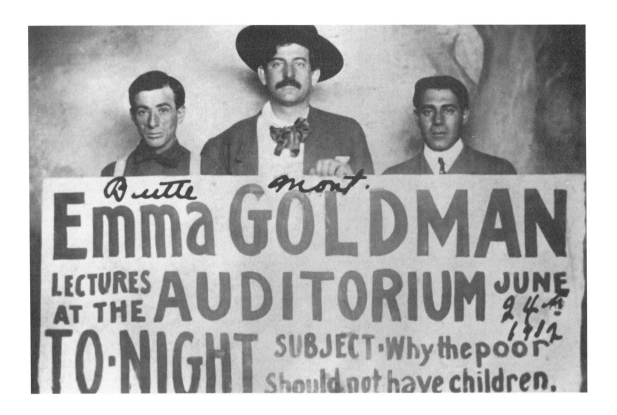

As an immigrant from Russia, Goldman arrived in America in 1885 with great hopes about American democracy. Her experience as an underpaid garment worker in upstate New York quickly led to disillusionment. She became further committed to workers' rights during the trial of the Haymarket Anarchists in Chicago. In 1886, when police tried to break up a labor demonstration of immigrant workers, a bomb exploded killing seven officers. Four anarchists (who came to be known as the "Haymarket Anarchists") were executed for the crime. In the aftermath of the trial and executions, nationwide awareness of worker unrest skyrocketed.

Determined to join the workers' uprising, Goldman moved to New York City later the same year. She became a popular and controversial public speaker, earning the nickname "Red Emma" for her radical ideas. In 1892 Goldman made an extremely unwise decision: she became involved in an assassination attempt against steel magnate Henry Frick during the Pittsburgh Steel Strike. Frick survived the attack; however, Goldman's

An advertisement for a Goldman birth control lecture in Butte, Montana, 1912.

The Comstock Law, 1873

During the 1870s antivice crusader (a vice is an action that leads to corruption or wickedness) Anthony Comstock led a campaign to prohibit the sending of obscene material through the mail. In 1873 Congress passed the Act for the Suppression of Trade in, and Circulation of, Obscene Literature and Articles of Immoral Use, which became known as the Comstock Law. The act banned the distribution of material that reformers feared might encourage immoral behavior. (Information about birth control and abortion fell into this category.) Anyone found guilty of violating the Comstock Law could be "imprisoned at hard labor in the penitentiary for not less than six months nor more than five years for each offence." Besides prison, a convicted person could also be fined between $100 to $2,000 and be forced to pay court costs.

For the next century the Comstock Law made it difficult for women and men to obtain contraceptives. In fact, many pioneers in the fight for birth control were arrested and sent to jail under the Comstock Law. Because of the efforts of Margaret Sanger, the courts determined in the early 1920s that birth control devices could be distributed as part of a program to prevent venereal disease.

associate, Alexander Berkman, received a 22-year prison sentence. Goldman later renounced violence when the assassin of President William McKinley claimed she had inspired him.

Goldman began lecturing about birth control in the early 1900s. She and other anarchists were the first people to challenge the 1873 Comstock Law, which prohibited the mailing of information about contraception and abortion. They felt the Comstock Law violated freedom of the press, an individual's right to privacy, and women's right to self-determination. At first Goldman only spoke about the issue of contraception and did not describe or teach actual methods to her audience. However, when activist Margaret Sanger was indicted (charged with a crime for her pro-birth control activities) and her magazine *Woman Rebel* banned, Goldman decided to distribute birth control information herself. She was arrested in New York City in February 1916 and used her trial as a public forum. After losing the case she refused to pay any fines and served 15 days in jail. Shortly after her release Goldman was arrested and then acquitted after giving another birth control speech.

Things to Remember While Reading "Victims of Morality":

- By prohibiting the mailing of obscene material, the Comstock Law of 1873 ignited an atmosphere of censorship throughout the nation. Information about contraception and abortion became illegal since they were listed as obscene under the law.

- Goldman attacks the law's originator, Anthony Comstock, and others who share the same "Morality." She felt that denying women the right to decide their own fate caused suffering at every stage of life, across all economic classes.

- Goldman highlights the economic, psychological, and social considerations women must face when deciding how many children to bring into the world.

Victims of Morality

Not so very long ago I attended a meeting addressed by Anthony Comstock, who has for forty years been the guardian of American morals. A more incoherent, ignorant ramble I have never heard from any platform.

The question that presented itself to me, listening to the commonplace, bigoted talk of the man, was, How could anyone so limited and unintelligent wield the power of censor and dictator over a supposedly democratic nation? True, Comstock has the law to back him. Forty years ago, when **puritanism** was even more rampant than to-day, completely shutting out the light of reason and progress, Comstock succeeded, through shady **machination** and political wire pulling, to introduce a bill which gave him complete control over the Post Office Department—a control which has proved disastrous

Puritanism: Doctrines of the Puritan religion; strict morals.

Machination: The act of plotting, usually with evil intentions.

to the freedom of the press, as well as the right of privacy of the American citizen.

Since then, Comstock has broken into the private chambers of people, has confiscated personal correspondence, as well as works of art, and has established a system of **espionage** and **graft** which would put Russia to shame. Yet the law does not explain the power of Anthony Comstock. There is something else, more terrible than the law. It is the narrow puritanic spirit, as represented in the sterile minds of the Young-Men-and-Old-Maid's Christian Union, Temperance Union, Sabbath Union, Purity League, etc. A spirit which is absolutely blind to the simplest manifestations of life; hence stands for stagnation and decay. As in **antebellum** days, these old fossils lament the terrible immorality of our time. Science, art, literature, the drama, are at the mercy of bigoted censorship and legal procedure, with the result that America, with all her boastful claims to progress and liberty is still steeped in the densest **provincialism**....

Unfortunately, the Lie of Morality still stalks about in fine feathers, since no one dares to come within hailing distance of that holy of holies. Yet [it] is safe to say that no other superstition is so detrimental to growth, so **enervating** and paralyzing to the minds and hearts of the people, as the superstition of Morality....

However, it is with the effect of Morality upon women that I am here mostly concerned. So disastrous, so paralyzing has this effect been, that some even of the most advanced among my sisters never thoroughly outgrow it.

It is Morality which condemns woman to the position of a **celibate**, a prostitute, or a reckless, **incessant** breeder of **hapless** children.

First, as to the celibate, the famished and withered human plant. When still a young, beautiful flower, she falls in love with a respectable young man. But Morality decrees that unless he can marry the girl, she must never know the raptures of love, the ecstasy of passion, which reaches its culminating expression in the sex

Espionage: Spying.
Graft: Dishonest gain.
Antebellum: Period of time before the Civil War.
Provincialism: Not sophisticated; characteristic of people from the provinces (rural areas) as opposed to people from cities (urban areas).
Enervating: Weakening; depriving of vitality.
Celibate: Someone who abstains from sexual intercourse.
Incessant: Continual.
Hapless: Unfortunate.

Goldman works on her
memoirs with an assistant,
1931.

embrace. The respectable young man is willing to marry, but the Property Morality, the Family and Social Moralities decree that he must first make his pile, must save up enough to establish a home and be able to provide for a family. The young people must wait, often many long, weary years.

Meanwhile the respectable young man, excited through the daily association and contact with his sweetheart, seeks an outlet for his nature in return for money [given to a prostitute]. In ninety-nine cases out of a hundred, he will be infected [with a sexually transmitted disease], and when he is materially able to marry, he will infect his wife and possible offspring. And the young flower, with every fiber aglow with the fire of life, with all her being crying out for love and passion? She has no outlet. She develops headaches, insomnia, hysteria; grows embittered, quarrelsome, and soon becomes a faded, withered, joyless being, a nuisance to herself and everyone else....

*Now, as to the prostitute. In spite of laws, ordinances, persecution, and prisons; in spite of segregation, registration, vice crusades, and other similar devices, the prostitute is the real **specter** of our age. She sweeps across the plains like a fire burning into every nook of life, devastating, destroying.*

*After all, she is paying back, in a very small measure, the curse and horrors society has strewn in her path. She ... is yet the **Nemesis** of modern times, the **avenging** angel, ruthlessly wielding the sword of fire. For has she not the man in her power? And, through him, the home, the child, the race. Thus she slays, and is herself the most brutally slain....*

*The prostitute is victimized by still other forces, foremost among them the Property Morality, which compels woman to sell herself as a sex commodity for a dollar per, out of wedlock, or for fifteen dollars a week, in the sacred fold of matrimony. The latter is no doubt safer, more respected, more recognized, but of the two forms of prostitution the girl of the street is the least **hypocritical,** the least **debased,** since her trade lacks the pious mask of hypocrisy; and yet she is hounded, fleeced, outraged, and shunned, by the very powers that have made her: the financier, the priest, the moralist, the judge, the jailor, and the detective, not to forget her sheltered, respectably virtuous sister, who is the most relentless and brutal in her persecution of the prostitute.*

*Morality and its victim, the mother—what a terrible picture! Is there indeed anything more terrible, more criminal, than our glorified sacred function of motherhood? The woman, physically and mentally unfit to be a mother, yet condemned to breed; the woman, economically taxed to the very last spark of energy, yet forced to breed; ... the woman, worn and used-up from the process of procreation, yet coerced to breed, more, ever more. What a hideous thing, this much-**lauded** motherhood! No wonder thousands of women risk mutilation, and prefer even death to this curse of the cruel imposition of the spook of Morality. Five thousand are yearly sacrificed upon the altar of this monster, that will not stand for prevention but*

Specter: Threatening or haunting possibility.

Nemesis: Greek goddess of vengeance.

Avenging: Taking revenge.

Hypocritical: Presenting a false impression.

Debased: Lowered in status or position.

Lauded: Praised; glorified.

Emma Goldman

Emma Goldman (1869-1940) was born in the Jewish ghetto of Kaunas, Lithuania, then part of the Russian empire. During her early teens she moved with her family to St. Petersburg, where she worked in her cousin's glove factory. In time she became involved in a radical movement known as Nihilism, which advocated violence to destroy oppressive organizations.

When anti-Jewish sentiment in Russia became a serious threat in the late nineteenth century, the family moved to Germany. To escape an arranged marriage, Goldman immigrated to the United States when she was 16 years old. Inspired by the trial of the Haymarket Anarchists in 1886, she began her political career by giving fiery public talks supporting the working class and opposing capitalism. (Capitalism is an economic system based on private—rather than government—ownership and on the distribution of goods in a free and competitive market.) Along with Alexander Berkman she founded the radical monthly magazine *Mother Earth* and served as its editor from 1906 to 1918. Goldman also published various books, including *Anarchism and Other Essays* (1911) and *The Significance of Modern Drama* (1914).

would cure by abortion. Five thousand soldiers in the battle for their physical and spiritual freedom, and as many thousands more who are crippled and mutilated rather than bring forth life in a society based on decay and destruction.

Is it because the modern woman wants to shirk responsibilities, or that she lacks love for her offspring, that she is driven to the most drastic and dangerous means to avoid bearing children? Only shallow, bigoted minds can bring such an accusation. Else they would know that the modern woman has become race-conscious, sensitive to the needs and rights of the child, as the unit of the race, and that therefore the modern woman has a sense of responsibility and humanity, which was quite foreign to her grandmother.

With the economic war raging all around her, with strife, misery, crime, disease, and insanity staring her in the face, with numberless little children ground into gold dust, how can the self- and race-conscious woman become a mother? Morality can not answer this question. It can only dictate, coerce, or condemn—and how many women are strong enough to face this condemnation, to defy the moral **dicta**? Few, indeed. Hence they fill the factories, the reformatories, the homes for feeble minded, the prisons, the insane asylums, or they die in the attempt to prevent child-birth. Oh, Motherhood, what crimes are committed in thy name! What hosts are laid at your feet, Morality, destroyer of life!

Fortunately, the Dawn is emerging from the chaos and darkness. Woman is awakening, she is throwing off the nightmare of Morality; she will no longer be bound. In her love for the man, she is not concerned in the contents of his pocketbook, but in the wealth of his nature, which alone is the fountain of life and joy. Nor does she need the sanction of the State. Her love is sanction enough for her. Thus she can abandon herself to the man of her choice, as the flowers abandon themselves to dew and light, in freedom, beauty, and ecstasy.

Through her re-born consciousness as a unit, a personality, a race builder, she will become a mother only if she desires the child, and if she can give to the child, even before its birth, all that her nature and intellect can yield: harmony, health, comfort, beauty, and, above all, understanding, reverence, and love, which is the only fertile soil for new life, a new being.

Morality has no terrors for her who has risen beyond good and evil. And though Morality may continue to devour its victims, it is utterly powerless in the face of the modern spirit, that shines in all its glory upon the brow of man and woman, liberated and unafraid. (Goldman, pp. 126-32)

What happened next...

Emma Goldman opposed America's involvement in World War I and was sentenced to prison in 1917 for antigovernment activities, namely protesting the draft. When released two years later she was deported to the Soviet Union along with 248 other people also associated with the postwar "Red Scare," a paranoid fear of communism that began sweeping through the United States after World War I. Although Goldman sympathized with the cause of communism, she took a stand against the Soviet government's heavy-handed power over its citizens. Her harsh criticism and book *My Disillusionment in Russia* (1923) shocked many of her fellow radicals. Goldman spent the rest of her life traveling and living in Canada and Europe. She always hoped one day she would be allowed to return to the United States, which she regarded as her chosen homeland.

Did you know...

- When Emma Goldman immigrated to the United States, she originally settled in Rochester, New York, where she worked in a coat factory and earned $2.50 a week. Her experiences as an underpaid immigrant worker contributed to her dissatisfaction with American democracy.

- Goldman worked as a nurse in 1893 while imprisoned for inciting a riot of unemployed workers in Union Square, New York City. After her release she traveled to Vienna, Austria, and received further training in midwifery and nursing.

- After being banished to the Soviet Union for her anti-American activities, Goldman later settled in France. She died in Toronto, Canada, in 1940 while on a fund-raising campaign in support of anti-Franco forces in the Spanish Civil War. (Francisco Franco was a Spanish general and dictator who ruled Spain with an iron hand for four decades.) The U.S. government granted her request to be buried in a Chicago cemetery beside the Haymarket Anarchists.

For Further Reading

Goldman, Emma. *Red Emma Speaks.* Compiled and edited by Alix Kates Shulman. New York: Random House, 1972.

Wexler, Alice. *Emma Goldman: An Intimate Life.* New York: Pantheon Books, 1984.

Birth Control in the Feminist Program, 1918

Britain's Labor Women, 1925

Selections from Crystal Eastman on Women and Revolution
Written by Crystal Eastman
Original essays collected and published together in 1978

Feminist and socialist labor lawyer Crystal Eastman was an early supporter of birth control rights. Born of suffragist parents (fighters for women's right to vote), Eastman devoted her entire life to overcoming socially imposed inequality. She challenged society's beliefs with a grace and style that impressed even her staunchest opponents. Her commitment to equality combined with her socialist beliefs (socialism is a political doctrine that champions the removal of private property in a quest to attain a classless society) placed her on the radical side of the women's rights movement of the early twentieth century.

Eastman and other intellectuals embraced socialism as a way to bring equality to everyone, regardless of class, race, or gender. They saw socialism as a process that would allow citizens to gain control over their own destiny. With considerable charisma, she championed both feminist and socialist causes by lecturing, writing, and working with political organizations. Her brother, the poet and socialist Max Eastman, once described her by saying, "She poured magnetic streams of generous love around her all the time."

Eastman developed an interest in labor law while studying for her law degree at New York University. After graduating in 1907 she worked with the Russell Sage Foundation to complete the first in-depth investigation of industrial accidents. Two years later, while serving as the only woman on the Employer's Liability Commission, she drafted New York's first worker's compensation law, which became the model followed by many other states. Her contributions to labor law and industrial safety received national and international acclaim.

As a dedicated feminist Eastman worked extensively with the National Woman's Party, a women's rights group associated with militant actions such as public parades and hunger strikes. Her commitment to pacifism, the belief that disputes could be settled peacefully, led her to help start the Woman's Peace Party (WPP) in 1915. With the war in Europe looming over America, Eastman and many other women's rights leaders worked together for international peace. When World War I ended the WPP joined its European counterparts to form the Women's International League for Peace and Freedom, which is still active today.

Eastman's brother Max was a famous poet and lecturer.

While many of her contemporaries focused solely on suffrage, Eastman believed women needed to achieve economic independence to experience full freedom. She saw the right to understand and use birth control as an essential requirement for women's true equality. Unlike many of her peers, Eastman also recognized that liberated women would have to juggle their desire for a family with their desire to work. With uncanny foresight she asked women to consider the crucial dilemma: "how to reconcile these two desires in real life, that is the question."

Things to Remember While Reading Eastman's Essays:

- Eastman believes women have a fundamental right to economic independence and birth control. She opposes the laws that prohibit doctors from instructing even married couples about how to limit the size of their families.

- She expresses concerns about the pressures on women to be "supermen" by having a career and homemaking responsibilities. Written in 1918, her article in the *Birth Control Review* foreshadows the challenges women would face in the latter part of the century.

- Notice Eastman optimistically assumes that once women win the right to vote, they will easily repeal anticontraception laws. Although women won the vote in 1920, more than 40 years would pass before the Supreme Court recognized a married couple's right to privacy and therefore to practice birth control.

Birth Control in the Feminist Program

*Feminism means different things to different people, I suppose. To women with a taste for politics and reform it means the right to vote and hold office. To women physically strong and adventuresome it means freedom to enter all kinds of athletic contests and games, to compete with men in aviation, to drive racing cars, ... to enter dangerous trades, etc. To many it means social and sex freedom, doing away with exclusively feminine virtues. To most of all it means economic freedom,—not the ideal economic freedom dreamed of by revolutionary **socialism,** but such economic freedom as it is possible for a human being to achieve under the existing system of competitive production and distribution,—in short such freedom to choose one's way of making a living as men now enjoy, and definite economic rewards for one's work when it happens to be "home-making." This is to me the central fact of*

Socialism: Political theory of a classless state in which government distributes goods and controls the means of production.

feminism. Until women learn to want economic independence, i.e., the ability to earn their own living independently of husbands, fathers, brothers or lovers,—and until they work out a way to get this independence without denying themselves the joys of love and motherhood, it seems to me feminism has no roots. Its manifestations are often delightful and stimulating but they are **sporadic,** they effect no lasting change in the attitude of men to women, or of women to themselves.

Whether other feminists would agree with me that the economic is the fundamental aspect of feminism, I don't know. But on this we are surely agreed, that Birth Control is an elementary essential in all aspects of feminism. Whether we are the special followers of Alice Paul [founder of the National Woman's Party] or Ruth Law, or Ellen Key, or Olive Schreiner [South African author known for her pro-women's rights and pacifist writings], we must all be followers of Margaret Sanger [pioneer in the birth control movement]. Feminists are not nuns. That should be established. We want to love and to be loved, and most of us want children, one or two at least. But we want our love to be joyous and free—not clouded with ignorance and fear. And we want our children to be deliberately, eagerly called into being, when we are at our best, not crowded upon us in times of poverty and weakness. We want this precious sex knowledge not just for ourselves, the conscious feminists; we want it for all the millions of unconscious feminists that swarm the earth,—we want it for all women.

Life is a big battle for the complete feminist even when she can regulate the size of her family. Women who are creative, or who have administrative gifts, or business ability, and who are ambitious to achieve and fulfill themselves in these lines, if they also have the normal desire to be mothers, must make up their minds to be a sort of supermen, I think. They must develop greater powers of concentration, a stronger will to "keep at it," a more determined ambition than men of equal gifts, in order to make up for the time and energy and thought and devotion that child-bearing, even in the most "advanced" fam-

Sporadic: Irregular.

Crystal Eastman

Crystal Eastman (1881-1928) was born in Marlborough, Massachusetts. She spent most of her childhood in Glenora on Seneca Lake, New York. Both her mother and father were ordained Congregational ministers and active suffragists who encouraged Eastman to develop her independence. She graduated from Vassar College in 1903 and received a master's degree in sociology from Columbia University the following year. After completing her law degree at New York University in 1907 (and ranking second in her class), she helped create the first worker's compensation law. Throughout her life Eastman was close to her brother, Max Eastman, a brilliant poet. Together they ran the socialist magazine *The Liberator* from 1918 to 1922.

---

ilies, seems ***inexorably*** to demand of the mother. But if we add to this handicap complete uncertainty as to when children may come, how often they come or how many there shall be, the thing becomes impossible. I would almost say that the whole structure of the feminist's dream of society rests upon the rapid extension of scientific knowledge about birth control.

This seems so obvious to me that I was astonished the other day to come upon a group of distinguished feminists who discussed for an hour what could be done with the woman's vote in New York State and did not once mention birth control.

As the readers of this magazine well know, the laws of this state, instead of establishing free clinics as necessary centers of information for the facts about sex hygiene and birth control, actually make it a crime, even on the part of a doctor, to tell grown men and women how to limit the size of their families. What could be a more pressing demand on the released energies of all these valiant suffrage workers than to repeal the law?

Inexorably: Relentlessly.

*This work should especially commend itself, now in wartime when so many kinds of reform are outlawed. There is nothing about Birth Control agitation to embarrass the President or obstruct the prosecution of the war.... It is a reform absolutely vital to the progress of woman and one which the war does not interfere with. While American men are fighting to rid the old world of **autocracy** let American women set to and rid the new world of this intolerable old burden of sex ignorance. It should not be a difficult task.*

*I don't believe there is one woman within the confines of this state who does not believe in birth control. I never met one. That is, I never met one who thought that she should be kept in ignorance of contraceptive methods. Many I have met ... valued the knowledge they possessed, but thought there were certain other classes who would be better kept in ignorance. The old would protect the young. The rich would keep the poor in ignorance. The good would keep their knowledge from the bad, the strong from the weak, and so on. But never in all my travels have I come on one married woman who, possessed of this knowledge would willingly part with it, or who not yet informed, was not eager for knowledge. It is only hypocrisy, and here and there a little hard-faced **puritanism** we have to overcome. No genuine human interest will be against the repeal of this law. Of course capitalism thrives on an oversupplied labor market, but with our usual enormous immigration to be counted on as soon as the war [World War I] is over, it is not likely that an organized economic opposition to birth control will develop.*

In short, if feminism, conscious and bold and intelligent, leads the demand, it will be supported by the secret eagerness of all women to control the size of their families, and a suffrage state should make short work of repealing these old laws that stand in the way of birth control. (Eastman, originally published in Birth Control Review, *January 1918, reprinted in* Crystal Eastman on Women and Revolution, *pp. 46-49)*

Autocracy: Rule by a single person with unlimited authority.

Puritanism: Doctrines of the Puritan religion; strict morals.

Privacy and Reproduction

Various legal decisions have helped clarify issues raised by the 1873 Comstock Law, which banned the distribution of material considered immoral (such as birth control). In the 1965 case of *Griswold vs. Connecticut,* the U.S. Supreme Court supported the right to privacy and therefore allowed the use of contraceptives by married couples. In a case heard seven years later, the Supreme Court again protected the right of privacy by overturning a Massachusetts law that prohibited the distribution of birth control to unmarried people (*Eisenstadt vs. Baird*).

The right to privacy in matters relating to reproduction also served as the basis of the most important ruling in the United States concerning abortion. The Supreme Court's decision in the historic *Roe vs. Wade* case secured the right for women to choose to have an abortion during the first three months of pregnancy. And exactly one hundred years after the passage of the Comstock Law, the Supreme Court determined a more specific definition of obscenity in *Miller vs. California* (1973).

Britain's Labor Women

... The birth-control resolution which was carried read:

This conference is of the opinion that it should be permissible for doctors employed in any medical service for which public funds are provided to give information on birth control to married people who desire it.

It is not illegal in England to distribute information in regard to contraceptives. The issue was whether the public health centers should do carefully and scientifically what so many women manage to do as best they can. Two years ago the subject was very timidly discussed. Last year Dora Russell and Freda Laski put through a resolution asking that the health centers give out such information, but the Roman Catholic Minister of Health in the Labor Government would not move.

This year no two women "put through" the resolution. The whole floor was for it, with a few bitter exceptions who regard contraceptives as a frustration of God and the moral order. However, "I am a Catholic," said a stout motherly woman, climbing on her chair as is the custom for speakers from the floor, "and I want to say that the Catholics better be honest. They are practicing birth control if they've got the information." To two firm young socialists who rose to explain that birth control was an economic issue that would not survive the social revolution an earnest woman replied firmly: "Even in the **cooperative commonwealth** *I think a woman will want to choose her time and say how many...." (Eastman, originally published in the* Nation, *July 15, 1925, reprinted in* Crystal Eastman on Women and Revolution, *pp. 141-43)*

What happened next...

Eastman found it difficult to secure regular work in the 1920s. Her radical pacifism and socialism during World War I left her without many opportunities during the conservative post-war era. In addition, her support of the Equal Rights Amendment (ERA) kept her from working in labor law, her original area of expertise. The ERA challenged the popular and newly secured protective legislation that regulated wages and hours for working women, but not for men. By arguing that protective legislation hurt the rights of women by setting them apart from men, Eastman alienated leaders from both labor and women's rights groups. During the last years of her life she divided her efforts between the American and English feminist and socialist movements.

Did you know...

• Eastman belonged to Heterodoxy, an unusual Saturday luncheon club based in New York City. Although not a secret

Cooperative commonwealth:
An ideal society based on the mutual cooperation of its people.

club, the group purposely did not record minutes, activities, or even its meeting places. Founded in 1912, the club consisted of leading professional feminist women who met to discuss political and social issues without fear of reprisal (meaning without fear of retaliation or revenge from opponents).

- Along with other women's rights advocates, Eastman supported a concept known as "motherhood endowment." Through a system of tax refunds, women who stay at home to raise their children would be "paid" for their work as mothers.

- A natural athlete and proponent of physical activity for women, Eastman frequently challenged conventional dress codes. As a young girl she preferred to wear a bathing suit without heavy stockings and a skirt—a decision that shocked her neighbors.

- Less than a year after the sudden death of her husband, Walter Fuller, Eastman died in 1928 of a kidney condition at the age of 46. Close friends of Eastman and Fuller adopted their two young children, Jeffrey and Annis.

For Further Reading

Birth Control Review, January 1918.

Eastman, Crystal. *Crystal Eastman on Women and Revolution.* Edited by Blanche Wiesen Cook. Oxford: Oxford University Press, 1978.

Nation, July 15, 1925.

Progress We Have Made

Selection from Woman and the New Race
Written by Margaret Sanger
Published in 1920

Margaret Sanger is considered the founder of the birth control movement in the United States. As a nurse working among poor immigrant families in New York City, Sanger saw firsthand the misery caused by unplanned pregnancies. She witnessed the suffering associated with poverty-induced hunger, the physical consequences of constant childbearing, and the often deadly effects of abortion attempts. While other activists worked for women's suffrage (the right to vote), Sanger became convinced that the right to reproductive autonomy (self-direction or freedom) was more urgent.

To help women learn about birth control, Sanger began publishing articles in the socialist weekly paper *The Call* in 1912. From the beginning she knew she faced considerable obstacles, including the risk of arrest. Information about birth control and abortion was considered obscene under the Comstock Law of 1873 and therefore illegal.

After traveling to Europe in 1914 to learn about the latest contraceptive methods, Sanger returned to New York ready to

Sanger returning from a trip to Europe in 1932.

embark on a full-blown campaign of birth control education. She launched a magazine titled the *Woman Rebel,* which supported feminism, socialism, and birth control. The magazine existed for only seven months before the United States Post Office denied Sanger's postal permit and indicted her (charged her with a crime) for violation of the Comstock Act. Sanger fled the country to escape arrest, but her husband, William

Roman Catholics and Contraception

In 1968 the leader of the Roman Catholic church, Pope Paul VI, issued the *Humanae Vitae,* a paper containing the official position of the church on the practice of birth control. The treatise stated that the Catholic church did not condone the use of any artificial means of birth control; rather, it only permitted "natural timing"—an estimation of a woman's fertile period and a couple's subsequent decision to refrain from having intercourse during that time in her cycle—as a means of family planning. For millions of Catholics, church doctrine on birth control (which was reaffirmed by Pope John Paul II in 1993) presents a serious challenge to their faith. After grappling with the emotional, physical, and financial implications of raising a large family in a modern world, some Catholics have come to terms with their personal decision to use modern birth control methods—and still consider themselves faithful members of the church.

Sanger, stayed in the States. In 1915 he was arrested for distributing her pamphlet *Family Limitation,* which contained detailed instructions for preventing pregnancy.

While in Europe, Sanger learned that her five-year-old daughter had died of pneumonia. Upon her return to New York City she received such strong public sympathy that the authorities decided to drop all charges against her. Determined to continue her crusade and to commemorate her daughter, Sanger opened the first birth control clinic in Brooklyn, New York, in 1916. Although she was arrested and spent a month in jail, she remained committed to her cause.

Sanger continued her mission by launching a new magazine, *Birth Control Review*, in 1917. She coined the term "birth control" in 1921, the same year she founded the American Birth Control League. Her tireless efforts to secure women's reproductive rights left a legacy of freedom for countless generations.

Things to Remember While Reading "Progress We Have Made":

- As a nurse working in the poor immigrant neighborhoods of New York City, Sanger observed the suffering of impoverished mothers trying their best to provide for their children. She herself was born into a family that had to struggle for its very existence, so she understood the need to prevent future pregnancies.

- In 1916 Sanger and her sister, Ethel Byrne, opened the nation's first birth control clinic in the Brownsville section of Brooklyn, New York. Before the police shut the clinic down, nearly five hundred women received birth control information in the course of ten days.

- Since birth control was considered obscene under the Comstock Law, the "birth control sisters" were arrested and spent a month in jail. Byrne's 11-day hunger strike won them considerable nationwide publicity.

- The judge at Sanger's appeal trial (meaning her case was heard in a higher court) ruled that physicians have the right to dispense birth control as a way to prevent venereal disease. This ruling made Sanger see that members of the medical profession could be her biggest potential allies. After 1917 she deliberately toned down her radical ways to gain the acceptance and powerful support of physicians.

Progress We Have Made

THE silence of the centuries has been broken. The wrongs of woman and the rights of woman have found voices. These voices differ from all others that have been raised in woman's behalf. They are not the individual protests of great feminine minds, nor the masculine remedies for masculine oppression.... Great voices are heard, both of women and of men, but intermingled with them are millions of voices demanding freedom....

*The walls of the **cloister** have fallen before the cries of a rising womanhood. The barriers of **prurient puritanism** are being demolished. Free woman has torn the veil of indecency from the secrets of life to reveal them in their power and their purity. Womanhood yet bound has beheld and understood. A public whose thoughts and opinions had been governed by men and by women engulfed in the old order has been shocked awake.*

*Sneers and jests at birth control are giving way to a reverent understanding of the needs of woman. They who to-day deny the right of a woman to control her own body speak with the **hardihood** of **invincible** ignorance or with the **folly** of those blind ones who in all ages have opposed the light of progress. Few there are to insist openly that woman remain a passive instrument of reproduction. The subject of birth control is being lifted out of the **mire** into which it was cast by puritanism and given its proper place among the sciences and the ideals of this generation. With this effort has come an illumination of all other social problems. Society is beginning to give ear to the promise of modern womanhood: "When you have ceased to chain me, I shall by the virtue of a free motherhood remake the world."*

It would be miraculous indeed if that victory which has been won, had been gained without great toil, insufferable

Cloister: *A place devoted to religious seclusion, such as a monastery or convent.*

Prurient: *Obsessive interest in sexual matters.*

Puritanism: *Doctrines of the Puritan religion; strict morals.*

Hardihood: *Boldness; daring.*

Invincible: *Unconquerable.*

Folly: *Foolishness; lack of good sense.*

Mire: *Soggy and muddy ground.*

anguish and sacrifice such as all persons experience when they dare to brave the conventions of the dead past or blaze a trail for a new order.

But where the vision is clear, the faith deep, forces unseen rally to assist and carry one over barriers which would otherwise have been insurmountable. No part of this wave of woman's emancipation has won its way without such vision and faith.

This is the one movement in which pioneering was unnecessary. The cry for deliverance always goes up. It is its own pioneer. The facts have always stared us in the face. No one who has worked among women can be ignorant of them. I remember that ever since I was a child, the idea of large families associated itself with poverty in my mind. As I grew to womanhood, and found myself working in hospitals and in the homes of the rich and the poor, the association between the two ideas grew stronger.

In every home of the poor, women asked me the same question. As far back as 1900, I began to inquire of my associates among the nurses what one could tell these worried women who asked constantly: "What can I do?" It is the voice of the elemental urge of woman—it has always been there; and whether we have heeded it or neglected it, we have always heard it. Out of this cry came the birth control movement....

When it came time to arouse new public interest in birth control and organize a movement, it was found **expedient** to employ direct and drastic methods to awaken a slumbering public. The Woman Rebel, a monthly magazine, was established to proclaim the gospel of revolt. When its mission was accomplished and the words "birth control" were on their way to be a symbol of woman's freedom in all civilized tongues, it went out of existence.

The deceptive "obscenity law," invoked oftener to repress womanhood and smother scientific knowledge than to restrain the distribution of verbal and pictorial pornography, was delib-

Expedient: Something adopted to meet an urgent need.

Sanger

The Population Bomb

Paul R. Ehrlich is a renowned biologist, natural scientist (one who studies matter and energy), and specialist in the study of insects, flies, and butterflies. In 1968 he wrote a revolutionary book, *The Population Bomb*. Using existing statistical information, Ehrlich projected that the human species—if allowed to continue at then-present rates of reproduction—would double every 25 years in underdeveloped countries and every 75 years in so-called "overdeveloped" countries (with modern industry, a healthy economy, and an educated populace) like the United States.

The Population Bomb points to world population growth as the cause of starvation, pollution, the rising crime rate, and a vast array of social problems. According to Ehrlich, the earth is gradually losing its ability to sustain the population's need for food, water, and other resources. The author proposes that global acceptance of the concept of "zero population growth" (in which the birth rate in a given area is not allowed to exceed the death rate) could help arrest this potentially disastrous trend.

erately challenged. This course had two purposes. It challenged the constitutionality of the law and thereby brought knowledge of contraceptives to hundreds of thousands of women.

The first general, organized effort reached in various ways to all parts of the United States. Particular attention was paid to the mining districts of West Virginia and Montana, the mill towns of New England and the cotton districts of the Southern states....

As time went on, the work was extended to various foreign elements of the population, this being made possible by the enthusiastic cooperation of workers who speak the foreign languages.

Leagues were formed to organized those who favored changing the laws. Lectures were delivered throughout the United States. Articles were written by eminent physicians, scientists, reformers and revolutionists. Debates were arranged. Newspapers and magazines of all kinds, classes and languages gave the subject of birth control serious attention, taking one side or the other of the discussion that was aroused. New books on the subject began to appear. Books by foreign authors were reprinted and distributed in the United States. The Birth Control Review, edited by voluntary effort and supported by a stock company of women who make contributions instead of taking dividends, was founded and continues its work.

After a year's study in foreign countries for the purpose of supplementing the knowledge gained in my fourteen years as a nurse, I came back to the United States determined to open a clinic. I had decided that there could be no better way of demonstrating to the public the necessity of birth control and the welcome it would receive than by taking the knowledge of contraceptive methods directly to those who needed it.

A clinic was opened in Brooklyn. There 480 women received information before the police closed the consulting rooms and arrested [Sanger's sister] Ethel Byrne, a registered nurse, Fania Mindell, a translator, and myself. The purpose of this clinic was to demonstrate to the public the practicability and the necessity of such institutions. All women who came seeking information were workingmen's wives. All had children. No unmarried girls came at all. Men came whose wives had nursing children and could not come.... [The] women invariably expressed their love for children, but voiced a common plea for means to avoid others, in order that they might give sufficient care to those already born....

For ten days the two rooms of this clinic were crowded to their utmost. Then came the police. We were hauled off to jail and eventually convicted of a "crime."

Ethel Byrne instituted a hunger strike for eleven days, which attracted attention throughout the nation. It brought to public notice the fact that women were ready to die for the prin-

Margaret Sanger

Margaret Sanger (1883-1966) was one of eleven children born to impoverished parents in Corning, New York. The physical toll of bearing so many children led her mother to an early death at the age of 49. Sanger's father expected the older siblings to help raise and support the large struggling family. With the funding provided by her two older sisters, Sanger graduated from Claverack College and then attended nursing school in White Plains, New York. Her experiences as a nurse working among the poor in New York City transformed her into a social radical and an advocate of birth control. For more than 50 years, Sanger campaigned tirelessly in the United States and abroad to help ensure that all women would have the ability to determine their own destiny. She lived long enough to see the administration of President Lyndon B. Johnson incorporate family planning into foreign and domestic public health and social welfare programs.

ciple of voluntary motherhood. So strong was the sentiment evoked that [the governor] ... pardoned Mrs. Byrne.

No single act of self-sacrifice in the history of the birth-control movement has done more to awaken the conscience of the public or to arouse the courage of women, than did Ethel Byrne's deed of uncompromising resentment at the outrage of jailing women who were attempting to disseminate *knowledge which would emancipate the motherhood of America.*

*Courage like hers and like that of others who have undergone arrest and imprisonment, or who night after night and day after day have faced street crowds to speak or to sell literature —the faith and the untiring labors of still others who have not come into public notice—have given the movement its **dauntless** character and assure the final victory.*

One dismal fact had become clear long before the Brownsville clinic opened. The medical profession as a whole had ignored the tragic cry of womanhood for relief from forced maternity. The private practitioners, one after another, shook their heads and replied: "It cannot be done. It is against the law," and the same answer came from clinics and public hospitals.

The decision of the New York State Court of Appeals has disposed of that objection, however, though as yet few physicians have cared to make public the fact that they take advantage of the decision.... Under the laws as they now stand in New York, any physician has a right to impart information concerning contraceptives to women as a measure for curing or preventing disease....

Forced thus to the front, the problems of birth control and the right of voluntary motherhood have been brought more and more to the attention of medical students, nurses, midwives, physicians, scientists and sociologists. A new literature, ranging all the way from discussion of the means of preventing conception to the social, political, ethical, moral and spiritual possibilities of birth control, is coming into being. Woman's cry for liberty is infusing itself into the thoughts and the consciences and the aspirations of the intellectual leaders as well as into the idealism of society....

And everywhere, serious-minded women and men, those with the vision, with a comprehension of present and future needs of society, are working to bring this message to those who have not yet realized its immense and regenerating import....

Dauntless: Fearless.

320 | Sanger

What does it all mean? It means that American woman-hood is blasting its way through the debris of crumbling moral and religious systems toward freedom. It means that the path is all but clear. It means that woman has but to press on, more courageously, more confidently, with her face set more firmly toward the goal. (Sanger, pp. 210-25)

What happened next...

In 1942 the American Birth Control League, which Margaret Sanger started in 1921, changed its name to the Planned Parenthood Federation of America. Over Sanger's objections, the ruling majority of the organization decided the term "planned parenthood" would sound more positive to Americans. The name change also reflected the broadened scope of medical services rendered by the clinics. Today the organization funds approximately 750 centers around the country. Continuing in the tradition originated by Sanger, Planned Parenthood provides women with information about contraception, sexually transmitted disease protection, abortion, sterilization, infertility, and menopause.

Did you know...

• In 1902 Sanger married her husband, William, an architect and artist, and together they had three children. When fire destroyed their newly built home, Sanger realized she could not base her happiness on material property. Determined to make a difference during her lifetime, she moved to New York City in 1908 and began working as a nurse.

• After World War II Sanger actively campaigned for a safe female-controlled contraceptive. Her financial, political, and administrative support for medical research helped lead to the development of the first birth control pill in 1960.

- In 1965, the year before her death, Sanger saw the Supreme Court strike down a remaining state law prohibiting the use of contraceptives. The case of *Griswold vs. Connecticut* recognized a married couple's right to privacy and therefore to use birth control freely—without having committed a crime.

For Further Reading

Gray, Madeline. *Margaret Sanger: A Biography of the Champion of Birth Control.* New York: Richard Marek Publishers, 1979.

Sanger, Margaret. *Woman and the New Race.* Originally published in 1920. New York: Maxwell Reprint Company, 1969.

Roe vs. Wade

United States Supreme Court Decision
Presented January 22, 1973

I n the landmark case of *Roe vs. Wade* the United States
Supreme Court declared that women have a constitutional
right to obtain an abortion (a procedure that terminates a
pregnancy). After two years of deliberation the court reached its
decision by a vote of seven to two, announcing its ruling on
January 22, 1973. Under the personal liberty clauses of the Ninth
and Fourteenth amendments, the Supreme Court justices ruled
that the government cannot interfere with a woman's universal
right to privacy. Since the practice of abortions had been legal
until the late 1800s, the *Roe vs. Wade* case in essence *re*legalized
abortion in America. At the time of the Supreme Court's decision
in 1973 most states prohibited abortion, except when the woman's
life was threatened by her pregnancy.

In 1970 a young pregnant woman in Texas using the pseudonym Jane Roe brought a class action suit (meaning it was on
behalf of herself and any other woman in a similar situation)
against Henry Wade, the district attorney of Dallas County. Roe
and her attorneys, Linda Coffee and Sarah Weddington, chal-

Justice Harry Blackmun (center) delivered the Supreme Court's majority opinion in Roe vs. Wade.

lenged the constitutionality of an 1857 state law that prevented women from having abortions except in extreme circumstances to save the mother's life. A lower court ruled in favor of Roe and overturned the Texas law; however, the process took too long to help Roe, who had her baby and gave it up for adoption. When Wade appealed (brought the case to a higher court for rehearing), the Supreme Court upheld the lower court's decision to strike down the Texas law.

Things to Remember While Reading the *Roe vs. Wade* Decision:

- Roe is considered the "appellant," meaning the person who made the original appeal or request. Her team of lawyers argue that women have a right to abortion based on the concept of personal liberty guaranteed in the Ninth and Fourteenth amendments to the Constitution. The Supreme Court agrees, concluding that the right of personal privacy includes the abortion decision.

- The Supreme Court notes that restrictive criminal abortion laws were passed within the nineteenth century, mainly to protect the health of the mother. (Abortion procedures were extremely crude and dangerous in the 1800s; safe antiseptic technique was not widely used until the turn of the twentieth century.)

- Wade is considered the "appellee," or the person an appeal is taken against. He and his legal representatives argue that the anti-abortion laws were designed to protect the rights of the unborn. While they suggest that the Constitution recognizes "fetus" in its use of the word "person," the court disagrees. However, the court does recognize the States' right to protect "potential" life, which they define at the point when a fetus becomes "viable," or able to survive outside of the mother's womb.

- The court establishes abortion regulations using a trimester framework. The state has no right to interfere during the first three months, or trimester, of pregnancy. During the second trimester, the state can regulate abortion only to protect the woman's health. Because the fetus is viable in the third trimester, the state may prohibit abortion unless the woman's health is in danger.

Roe vs. Wade

The principal thrust of **appellant**'s attack on the Texas statutes is that they improperly invade a right, said to be possessed by the pregnant woman, to choose to terminate her pregnancy. Appellant would discover this right in the concept of personal "liberty" embodied in the Fourteenth Amendment's **Due Process** Clause; or in personal, marital, familial, and sexual privacy said to be protected by the Bill of Rights ...; or

Appellant: One who appeals a court decision.

Due process: Use of the court system to protect one's legal rights.

among those rights reserved to the people by the Ninth Amendment.... Before addressing this claim, we feel it desirable briefly to survey, in several aspects, the history of abortion, for such insight as that history may afford us, and then to examine the state purposes and interests behind the criminal abortion laws.

It perhaps is not generally appreciated that the restrictive criminal abortion laws in effect in a majority of States today are of relatively recent **vintage.** Those laws, generally **proscribing** abortion or its attempt at any time during pregnancy except when necessary to preserve the pregnant woman's life, are not of ancient or even of **common-law** origin. Instead, they derive from statutory changes effected, for the most part, in the latter half of the 19th century....

[At] the time of the adoption of our Constitution, and throughout the major portion of the 19th century, abortion was viewed with less disfavor than under most American statutes currently in effect. Phrasing it another way, a woman enjoyed a substantially broader right to terminate a pregnancy than she does in most States today. At least with respect to the early stage of pregnancy....

Three reasons have been advanced to explain historically the enactment of criminal abortion laws in the 19th century and to justify their continued existence.

It has been argued occasionally that these laws were the product of a Victorian social concern to discourage illicit sexual conduct. Texas, however, does not advance this justification in the present case, and it appears that no court or commentator has taken the argument seriously. The appellants and **amici** contend, moreover, that this is not a proper state purpose at all and suggest that, if it were, the Texas statutes are overbroad in protecting it since the law fails to distinguish between married and unwed mothers.

A second reason is concerned with abortion as a medical procedure. When most criminal abortion laws were first enact-

Vintage: Age.
Proscribing: Prohibiting.
Common-law: Laws and customs developed in England and used in American colonies.
Amici: Latin for "friends," meaning "friends of the court."

Operation Rescue

In the heated controversy surrounding reproductive rights, those individuals who oppose a woman's right to obtain an abortion are said to take a "pro-life" stand. Basing their case on ethical, religious, and biological grounds, pro-life supporters maintain that embryos (the products of the early stages of pregnancy) are indeed alive, regardless of the degree of their development. The pro-life group with the highest profile in America is called Operation Rescue (OR). Formed in 1986 by Randall Terry, Operation Rescue opposes the concept of legal abortion on the grounds that the unborn are children in the eyes of God—and termination of a pregnancy at any stage is willful murder. OR members believe that they have a moral obligation to oppose the practice of abortion. The group targets selected abortion clinics and doctors' offices and attempts to shut them down by organizing protests, intimidating prospective patients, and setting up blockades to discourage women from entering the facilities. Many OR members have been arrested and taken to jail over the years, usually charged with criminal trespass. Rescuers justify their actions by reasoning that the law of God obligates them to protect the lives of the unborn, even if that involves breaking laws created by man.

ed, the procedure was a hazardous one for the woman. This was particularly true prior to the development of **antisepsis.** Antiseptic techniques, of course, were based on discoveries by [British surgeon Joseph] Lister, [French microbiologist Louis] Pasteur, and others first announced in 1867, but were not generally accepted and employed until about the turn of the century. Abortion **mortality** was high…. Thus, it has been argued that a State's real concern in enacting a criminal abortion law was to protect the pregnant woman, that is, to restrain her from submitting to a procedure that placed her life in serious jeopardy.

Modern medical techniques have altered this situation. Appellants and various amici refer to medical data indicating that abortion in early pregnancy, that is, prior to the end of the first **trimester,** although not without its risk, is now relatively safe.

Antisepsis: Destruction of microorganisms or germs that cause disease.

Mortality: Death, in this case to the pregnant woman.

Trimester: Three months.

Mortality rates for women undergoing early abortions, where the procedure is legal, appear to be as low as or lower than the rates for normal childbirth. Consequently, any interest of the State in protecting the woman from an inherently hazardous procedure, except when it would be equally dangerous for her to forgo it, has largely disappeared. Of course, important state interests in the areas of health and medical standards do remain. The State has a legitimate interest in seeing to it that abortion, like any other medical procedure, is performed under circumstances that insure maximum safety for the patient.... Moreover, the risk to the woman increases as her pregnancy continues. Thus, the State retains a definite interest in protecting the woman's own health and safety when an abortion is proposed at a late stage of pregnancy.

The third reason is the State's interest—some phrase it in terms of duty—in protecting **prenatal** life. Some of the argument for this justification rests on the theory that a new human life is present from the moment of conception. The State's interest and general obligation to protect life then extends, it is argued, to prenatal life. Only when the life of the pregnant mother herself is at stake, balanced against the life she carries within her, should the interest of the embryo or fetus not prevail. Logically, of course, a legitimate state interest in this area need not stand or fall on acceptance of the belief that life begins at conception or at some other point prior to live birth. In assessing the State's interest, recognition may be given to the less rigid claim that as long as at least potential life is involved, the State may assert interests beyond the protection of the pregnant woman alone.

Parties challenging state abortion laws have sharply disputed in some courts the contention that a purpose of these laws, when enacted, was to protect prenatal life. Pointing to the absence of legislative history to support the contention, they claim that most state laws were designed solely to protect the woman. Because medical advances have lessened this concern, at least with respect to abortion in early pregnancy, they

Prenatal: Before birth.

| Roe vs. Wade

argue that with respect to such abortions the law can no longer be justified by any state interest. There is some scholarly support for this view of original purpose....

It is with these interests, and the weight to be attached to them, that this case is concerned.

The Constitution does not explicitly mention any right of privacy. In a line of decisions, however, ... the Court has recognized that a right of personal privacy, or a guarantee of certain areas or zones of privacy, does exist under the Constitution....

This right of privacy, whether it be founded in the Fourteenth Amendment's concept of personal liberty and restrictions upon state action, as we feel it is, or ... in the Ninth Amendment's reservation of rights to the people, is broad enough to encompass a woman's decision whether or not to terminate her pregnancy.... We, therefore, conclude that the right

Anti-abortion protestors stage a demonstration in Washington, DC.

Reproductive Rights | 329

Sarah Weddington was one of two attorneys who represented Jane Roe in her class action suit.

of personal privacy includes the abortion decision, but that this right is not unqualified and must be considered against important state interests in regulation....

The **appellee** and certain amici argue that the fetus is a "person" within the language and meaning of the Fourteenth Amendment. In support of this, they outline at length and in detail the well-known facts of fetal development.... The Constitution does not define "person" in so many words.... But in nearly all ... instances, the use of the word is such that it has application only postnatally. None indicates, with any assurance, that it has any possible prenatal application.... In short, the unborn have never been recognized in the law as persons in the whole sense.

In view of all this, we do not agree that, by adopting one theory of life, Texas may override the rights of the pregnant woman that are at stake. We repeat, however, that the State does have an important and legitimate interest in preserving and protecting the health of the pregnant woman ... and that it has still another important and legitimate interest in protecting the potentiality of human life. These interests are separate and distinct. Each grows in **substantiality** as the woman approaches term and, at a point during pregnancy, each becomes "compelling."

With respect to the State's important and legitimate interest in the health of the mother, the "compelling" point, in the light of present medical knowledge, is at approximately the end of the first trimester. This is so because of the now-established medical fact ... that until the end of the first trimester mortality in abortion may be less than mortality in normal childbirth.... It follows that, from and after this point, a State may regulate the abortion procedure to the extent that the regulation rea-

Appellee: The person an appeal is taken against.
Substantiality: Considerable importance.

Roe vs. Wade

sonably relates to the preservation and protection of maternal health.... This means, on the other hand, that for the period of pregnancy prior to this "compelling" point, the attending physician, in consultation with his patient, is free to determine, without regulation by the State, that, in his medical judgment, the patient's pregnancy should be terminated....

*With respect to the State's important and legitimate interest in potential life, the "compelling" point is at **viability**. This is so because the fetus then presumably has the capability of meaningful life outside the mother's womb. State regulation protective of fetal life after viability thus has both logical and biological justifications. If the State is interested in protecting fetal life after viability, it may go so far as to proscribe abortion during that period, except when it is necessary to preserve the life or health of the mother....*

Our conclusion ... means, of course, that the Texas abortion statutes, as a unit, must fall. (Justice Blackmun, delivering the opinion of the United States Supreme Court as documented in Supreme Court Reporter, *Volume 93)*

What happened next...

Since the landmark *Roe vs. Wade* decision in 1973, the United States Supreme Court has heard several cases to further clarify abortion rights and limitations. While the court continues to uphold a woman's right to privacy and to abortion, several adjustments have been made. Based on Supreme Court rulings, states have the right to impose 24-hour waiting periods and to require minors to obtain parental or guardian permission before an abortion procedure is performed. Also, in the controversial 1989 decision *Webster vs. Reproductive Services* the court banned all abortions at public hospitals and prohibited the use of public funds toward abortions. Today the debate on abortion rights in America continues with both right-to-life and pro-choice advo-

Viability: Capable of living.

Norma McCorvey

Norma McCorvey (pseudonym for Jane Roe; 1947–) was born in Letteworth, Louisiana. When she found out she was pregnant in 1969, she was single and struggling to make a living. At the time abortion was considered illegal under Texas law, so McCorvey agreed to participate in a class action suit to try to change that law. Raised as a Jehovah's Witness (members of an evangelical group known for their extremist beliefs and literal interpretations of the laws of God), McCorvey chose to use the name Jane Roe in the case to avoid upsetting her father.

The legal process moved too slow to help McCorvey, who gave birth to a girl and arranged for her adoption. McCorvey chose to reveal her identity in 1984 and became involved with the pro-choice movement. She wrote a book about her experiences called *I Am Roe: My Life, Roe vs. Wade, and Freedom of Choice* (1994). Then, in 1995 she claimed to have had a profound religious experience and joined Operation Rescue, a pro-life organization.

cates holding rallies, organizing petition drives, and campaigning for political candidates.

Did you know...
- Norma McCorvey (Jane Roe) lost touch with her lawyers before the Supreme Court decided her case in 1973. She

learned about the court's decision while watching a television news program.

- In rendering its decision, the Supreme Court considered a pregnant woman's physical and mental health and the possible negative effects that an unwanted child might have on her life.

- The same day the Supreme Court issued its decision concerning *Roe vs. Wade,* it also ruled on a second abortion case known as *Doe v. Bolton.* The two decisions comprise the court's ruling to relegalize abortion. Some historians use the term "*Roe vs. Wade*" to refer to both cases.

For Further Reading

Faux, Marian. *Roe vs. Wade: The Untold Story of the Landmark Supreme Court Decision That Made Abortion Legal.* New York: Macmillan, 1988.

McCorvey, Norma, with Andy Meisler. *I Am Roe: My Life, Roe vs. Wade, and Freedom of Choice.* New York: HarperCollins, 1994.

Supreme Court Reporter. Volume 93. St. Paul, Minnesota: West Publishing Company, 1974.

Women's Voices: A Timeline of Events

Sojourner Truth

1790 Judith Sargent Murray publishes "On the Equality of the Sexes."

1792 Mary Wollstonecraft writes *A Vindication of the Rights of Women.*

1819 Emma Willard outlines her plan for female education.

1836 Sarah Bagley leaves home to become a "mill girl."

1836 Ernestine Rose begins to campaign for a married woman's property bill in New York state.

1838 Sarah Grimké composes her *Letters on the Equality of the Sexes.*

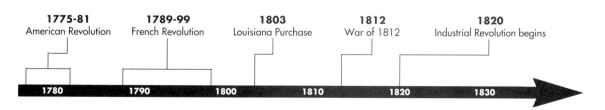

1775-81 American Revolution	**1789-99** French Revolution	**1803** Louisiana Purchase	**1812** War of 1812	**1820** Industrial Revolution begins
1780	1790	1800	1810	1820	1830

1840   Lucretia Mott is not allowed to participate in the World Anti-Slavery Convention in London, England.

1841   Catherine Beecher writes her best-selling book *A Treatise on Domestic Economy*.

1848   Elizabeth Cady Stanton presents her "Declaration of Sentiments" at the first Woman's Rights Convention in Seneca Falls, New York.

1848   Frederick Douglass publishes a supportive article about women's rights in his abolitionist newspaper *The North Star.*

1851   Sojourner Truth delivers her most famous speech "Ain't I a Woman?"

1855   Lucy Stone and Henry Blackwell protest the legal status of married women in their wedding vows.

1861   Julia Ward Howe writes "The Battle Hymn of the Republic."

1865   Thirteenth Amendment abolishes slavery in the United States.

1868   Fourteenth Amendment extends the scope of the Bill of Rights to matters under state jurisdiction.

1869   The National Woman Suffrage Association and the American Woman Suffrage Association are formed.

1869   John Stuart Mill writes *The Subjection of Women.*

1870   Fifteenth Amendment grants voting rights to black men.

1871   Victoria Woodhull argues before Congress that women have the right to vote.

1872   Susan B. Anthony and a group of 16 women are arrested for attempting to vote in the presidential election.

1873   Anthony Comstock helps win passage of the Comstock Law which outlaws the distribution of information about birth control and abortion.

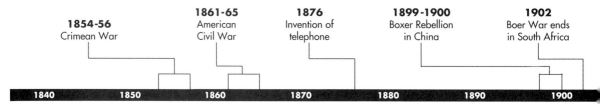

1854-56 Crimean War

1861-65 American Civil War

1876 Invention of telephone

1899-1900 Boxer Rebellion in China

1902 Boer War ends in South Africa

1840   1850   1860   1870   1880   1890   1900

1878 Francis Willard conducts her first petition drive for "Home Protection."

1889 Jane Addams organizes a settlement house to help poor immigrants in Chicago.

1896 The Supreme Court's *Plessy vs. Ferguson* ruling establishes the "separate but equal" policy of racial segregation.

1898 Charlotte Perkins Gilmore writes *Women and Economics.*

1900 Carrie Chapman Catt assumes her first term as president of the NAWSA.

1911 A fire at the Triangle Shirtwaist Factory kills 146 female workers.

c.1913 Ida B. Wells-Barnett helps form the first black women's suffrage organization, the Alpha Suffrage Club.

1916 Margaret Sanger opens the first birth control clinic in America.

1916 Emma Goldman is arrested for distributing information about birth control.

1918 Crystal Eastman discusses economic independence and birth control in *The Birth Control Review.*

1920 Nineteenth Amendment grants women the right to vote.

1923 Alice Paul introduces the first Equal Rights Amendment.

1929 Virginia Woolf writes *A Room of One's Own.*

1939-45 Thousands of women go to work in non-traditional factory and military jobs.

1948 United Nations delegate Eleanor Roosevelt plays pivotal role in the adoption of the Universal Declaration of Human Rights.

1953 Simone de Beauvoir publishes *The Second Sex* in English.

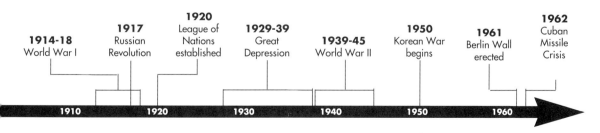

1914-18 World War I

1917 Russian Revolution

1920 League of Nations established

1929-39 Great Depression

1939-45 World War II

1950 Korean War begins

1961 Berlin Wall erected

1962 Cuban Missile Crisis

1910 1920 1930 1940 1950 1960

1954	The Supreme Court rules that segregation in schools is unconstitutional in *Brown vs. Board of Education.*
1963	Equal Pay Act guarantees women "equal pay for equal work."
1963	Betty Friedan writes *The Feminine Mystique.*
1964	Civil Rights Act assures all citizens freedom from discrimination based on race, color, religion, sex, or national origin.
1966	National Organization for Women is founded to promote full equality for both women and men
1968	Pope Paul VI issues *Humanae Vitae* forbidding Roman Catholics from using modern methods of birth control.
1971	Gloria Steinem and other women help create *Ms.* magazine.
1972	Both Houses of Congress pass the Equal Rights Amendment.
1973	The Supreme Court decision *Roe vs. Wade* legalizes abortion.
1982	Phyllis Schlafly's organization "Stop ERA" contributes to the defeat of the Equal Rights Amendment.
1986	Randall Terry starts the pro-life organization Operation Rescue.
1991	Civil Rights Act prohibits sexual harassment on the job.
1993	The Family and Medical Leave Act grants workers unpaid leave to take care of family emergencies.
1994	Shannon Faulkner applies to the Citadel, an all-male military college in South Carolina.
1996	The Virginia Military Institute is ordered to begin accepting women.

Photo Credits

Sarah Grimké

The photographs appearing in *Women's Voices: A Documentary History of Women in America* were received from the following sources:

On the cover (from top): Gloria Steinem (**Courtesy of Gloria Steinem. Reproduced by permission.**); Suffragist (**Courtesy of the Cleveland Public Library. Reproduced by permission.**); Ida B. Wells-Barnett (**Courtesy of the University of Chicago. Reproduced by permission.**).

The Granger Collection. Reproduced by permission.: pp. v, 41, 54, 115, 137, 147, 196; **Brown Brothers. Reproduced by permission.**: pp. xi, 121, 132; **Schlesinger Library, Radcliffe College. Reproduced by permission.**: pp. xv, 203; **National Portrait Gallery, Smithsonian Institution. Reproduced by permission.**: pp. 1, 79, 155, 335; **Sargent House Museum, Gloucester, MA. Reproduced by permission.**: pp. 5, 10; **UPI/Corbis-Bettmann. Reproduced by permission.**: pp. 19, 37, 85, 102, 239, 276, 285, 297, 324, 327, 330, 332; **Archive Photos. Reproduced by permis-**

sion.: pp. 23, 30, 75, 118, 155, 191, 232, 335; **Emma Willard School. Reproduced by permission.**: p. 27; **Harriet Beecher Stowe Center. Reproduced by permission.**: p. 33; **Friends Historical Society. Reproduced by permission.**: p. 50; **Courtesy of the Library of Congress:** pp. 63, 72, 82, 89, 130, 141, 159, 171, 209, 224, 339; **AP/Wide World Photos. Reproduced by permission.**: pp. 108, 112, 215, 218, 222, 225, 243, 253, 259, 263, 268, 279, 285, 286, 289, 303, 312, 313, 319; **Courtesy of the University of Chicago. Reproduced by permission.**: 150; **Museum of Textile History. Reproduced by permission.**: pp. 176, 180; **U.S.A.F. Museum. Courtesy of Hugh Morgan.**: p. 200; **Courtesy of the University of Illinois at Chicago, The University Library, Department of Special Collections, Jane Addams Memorial collection. Reproduced by permission.**: p. 206; **Courtesy of the University of Illinois at Chicago, The University Library, Department of Special Collections, Ben Reitman Papers. Reproduced by permission.**: p. 293.

Index

Bold type indicates main documents and speaker profiles

Italic type indicates volume numbers

Illustrations are marked by (ill.)

Lucy Stone

A

O

P